The Wonder of Consciousness

The Wonder of Consciousness: Understanding the Mind through Philosophical Reflection

Harold Langsam

The MIT Press

Cambridge, Massachusetts

London, England

For information about special quantity discounts, please e-mail special_sales@mitpress.mit.edu

W. D. Snodgrass, excerpt from "April Inventory" from *Not for Specialists: New and Selected Poems*. Copyright © 1959, 2003 by W. D. Snodgrass. Reprinted with the permission of BOA Editions, Ltd., www.boaeditions.org.

This book was set in Stone Sans and Stone Serif by the MIT Press. Printed and bound in the United States of America.

Library of Congress Cataloging-in-Publication Data
Langsam, Harold L., 1961–.
The wonder of consciousness : understanding the mind through philosophical reflection / Harold Langsam.
    p.   cm.
Includes bibliographical references (p.   ) and index.
ISBN 978-0-262-01585-1 (hardcover : alk. paper)
1. Consciousness. I. Title.
B808.9.L36   2011
126—dc22
                                                    2010045903

10 9 8 7 6 5 4 3 2 1

To Marcia

Though trees turn bare, and girls turn wives,
We shall afford our costly seasons;
There is a gentleness survives
That will outspeak and has its reasons.
There is a loveliness exists,
Preserves us, not for specialists.

—W. D. Snodgrass

Contents

Preface

I am privileged to be a philosopher; I get to sit in my study and think about the world in an attempt to gain knowledge of it. Of course there are many things about the world that you can discover only by going out and investigating it. But we philosophers tend to think that some of the most interesting features of the world are available for discovery merely by staying at home and engaging in careful reflection. This book is my modest attempt to describe what I believe I have discovered about the mind by staying home.

Thanks so much to Brie Gertler for discussion and detailed comments on the first three chapters. Thanks so much to Dan Moseley for detailed comments on the entire manuscript.

Thanks for support from the University of Virginia, which allowed me to take paid leave during the spring 2005 semester and begin writing this manuscript.

Thanks to my teachers at the Yeshivah of Flatbush for encouraging independent thought. Thanks especially to my ninth-grade English teacher Rhona Bar-Chama for teaching me how to write.

Thanks to all my philosophy professors at Princeton University, but thanks especially to my dissertation advisers Gil Harman and the late Margaret Wilson. Thanks to Gil for his humor and for reminding me that it's only philosophy. Thanks to Margaret for being the first (when I was an undergraduate student) to suggest that I consider graduate school in philosophy, and also for being the first (when I was a graduate student) to make me revise a paper.

Thanks to my parents Norman Langsam and Gloria Langsam for teaching me to do what I love. Thanks to my sisters Rosalee Lovett and Dr. Sharon Kuebbing for their lifelong love and support. Thanks to my wonderful daughter Emma Ruth Langsam for being exactly who you are. And special thanks to my wife Marcia Retchin Langsam for everything else (you).

1 Introduction

1.1 Wonder and Intelligibility

Consciousness is a wonderful thing. Let me say it again: consciousness is a wonderful thing; it amazes us, it fascinates us, it fills us with wonder. I don't mean to belabor the obvious here—well, no, I take that back; I do mean to belabor what I hope is an obvious feature of consciousness. We are generally so busy living our conscious lives that we fail to notice the wonder of consciousness. But it is not difficult to notice it; a moment of reflection is all it takes to recognize what I hope is obvious to everyone. And we *should* notice it; we should take the time to appreciate and celebrate the wonder of consciousness. But if we are fully to appreciate the wonder of consciousness, we need to articulate what it is about consciousness that makes it so wonderful. It is easy to notice that consciousness is wonderful; it is more difficult to articulate what the wonder of consciousness consists in. This book is an attempt at such an articulation.

Of course, consciousness is not the only wonderful thing in the world, but consciousness is wonderful in distinctive ways. The physical world studied by the natural sciences is wonderful; in fact, the more science teaches us about the physical world, the more wonderful that world seems to be. Science tells us about the hidden components and causes of observable physical phenomena, and what is so amazing about the physical world is how a small number of different kinds of hidden physical components and laws of nature are able to explain the wide variety of phenomena that make up the physical world. It is the hidden organization of the physical world that evokes wonder. But what is wonderful about consciousness is not to be found in its hidden nature or causes; it is right there on the surface. What is wonderful about consciousness is how its manifest features relate to each other. Specifically, what is wonderful is that these manifest features are such that we can know a priori that they stand in certain kinds of relations with each other. Typically, facts about the world cannot be known a priori, but consciousness is special: there are important facts about consciousness that can be known a priori.

I use the word "intelligible" to describe facts that can be known a priori. The idea here is that if a fact can be known a priori, something about the nature of that fact must explain why it can be known a priori; to describe a fact as *intelligible* is to say that it has the kind of nature that enables it to be known a priori. The use of this word seems appropriate because to know something a priori is to know it solely through the use of reason (intelligence), and perhaps a fact must in some sense exist in accordance with reason (be intelligible) if it is to be capable of being known by reason. I also say that a *thing* or *quality* or *feature* is intelligible when there are substantive facts about that thing or quality or feature that can be known a priori.[1]

In this book, I shall argue that consciousness is intelligible: there are substantive facts about consciousness that can be known a priori. I do not claim that all facts about consciousness can be known a priori; some facts about consciousness can be known only through introspection, and some facts about consciousness can be known only through scientific investigation. Nevertheless I claim that there are important facts about consciousness that can be known a priori, and I also suggest that the very intelligibility of consciousness is the source of its wonder.

The intelligibility of consciousness distinguishes it from phenomena that do not involve consciousness. We cannot learn anything substantive about the aspects of the world that do not involve consciousness merely by thinking about them. Rather, we learn about them by employing our senses to discover new things about them; through our senses we learn the nature of these new phenomena, how they relate to each other, and how they relate to the phenomena we already know about. There is nothing intelligible in the relevant sense about any of these phenomena; that's why we cannot discover them through employing our reason in the activity of thinking. But we can discover things about consciousness through reflective thinking. Specifically, given that we already know certain features of consciousness, reason can inform us of some of the relations between these features, for some of these relations are intelligible relations, and therefore reason can detect them.[2] (The relations are intelligible in the sense that it is an intelligible fact that the features in question stand in these relations.) We can learn things about consciousness merely by thinking about it, and surely that is a wonderful thing.

Consider the matter of causation, for example. As far as reason is concerned, any physical event can cause any other physical event; therefore we need to observe the physical world to discover the actual causes and effects of physical phenomena.[3] But consciousness is different; I argue in chapter 3 that mere reflection on the intrinsic nature of consciousness can inform us of some of the causal powers of consciousness, for the relations between these causal powers and the intrinsic features that ground them are intelligible relations. We might say that these causal powers of consciousness *flow* in an intelligible way from the relevant intrinsic features of consciousness: what consciousness can *do* is an intelligible function of what consciousness *is*.

I have suggested that the intelligibility of consciousness is the source of its wonder, and I can defend this suggestion only through the detailed examination of the intelligible facts about consciousness that I undertake in this book. But I can say right now that something about the phenomenon of intelligibility itself is apt to fill us with wonder. We are beings that possess a faculty of reason, and our use of this faculty is a major element of our lives. Let me suggest that the function of the faculty of reason is to detect and understand intelligible relations. Typically, we employ our reason in the activity of *reasoning*. When we reason, we are searching for intelligible relations between *propositions*. Perhaps we are thinking about what we can justifiably conclude on some matter based on what we already know, where a justifiable conclusion is just a proposition that stands in a relevant kind of intelligible relation to the propositions we already know.[4] Given that reasoning is the typical employment of reason, we are apt to think that intelligibility is typically to be found in relations among propositions. And insofar as we think of propositions as "abstract" entities, as entities whose existence is somewhat removed from the concrete spatiotemporal world in which we live, we are inclined to think that intelligibility is not typically to be found in our own concrete world. This thought seems confirmed by the fact that we do not find intelligibility in the nonmental aspects of our concrete world. So when we do find intelligibility in our world, specifically in the relations between features of consciousness, we are surprised and filled with wonder. We are amazed that there are elements of our concrete world that *make sense*, so to speak, that exist in accordance with reason.

So intelligibility by its very nature is a wonderful thing, but I think that the intelligibility of consciousness is wonderful for another reason. Consciousness is wonderful in virtue of its intelligibility, and insofar as consciousness is an element of our lives, our lives will share the wonder of consciousness. But other elements of our lives are wonderful, also. For example, we are rational beings, and we are also beings capable of knowledge. Not only can we obtain knowledge of the world through perceiving it, but through our emotional reactions to the world we can come to desire what is of value in the world, and thereby participate in this value. In chapters 4 and 5, I argue that consciousness is a necessary condition for these other wonderful elements of human life. Moreover, I argue that any account of why consciousness is needed for the presence of these other wonderful elements of human life must refer specifically to the intelligibility of consciousness. So the intelligibility of consciousness is wonderful not merely because the intelligibility of anything is wonderful but because the intelligibility of consciousness helps to explain the presence of other wonderful things in human life. Consciousness is important to us, both for its own sake and because it makes possible so many of the wonderful and worthwhile elements of our lives.

1.2 Intelligibility and Philosophy

My task here is to describe what it is about consciousness that makes it wonderful. What makes consciousness wonderful is its intelligibility. So my task is to describe the intelligible facts about consciousness. This task is a philosophical task. So in this book I give a philosophical description of consciousness.

The task of describing the intelligible facts about consciousness is a philosophical task because, as we have seen, it is a task for our faculty of reason, and philosophy is a discipline that seeks knowledge through the employment of reason. It is an a priori discipline. Philosophy distinguishes itself from science precisely in this respect: whereas the scientist seeks knowledge of the world through empirical investigation, the philosopher seeks knowledge of the world solely through the employment of reason. The force of this "solely" should be understood with some care. The philosopher is not interested in ignoring the known empirical facts about the world, whether they are facts that have been obtained through everyday perception and intro- spection or through scientific investigation. Rather, the point is that the philosopher seeks answers to questions that do not seem to require *further* empirical investigation; they merely seem to require reflection (by reason) on empirical facts we already know. Philosophizing begins when we find something puzzling about familiar facts, and we seek to remove our puzzlement by employing our reason to discover intelligibility in these facts.

Philosophy is not the only a priori discipline, but I think it is fairly characterized as the a priori discipline that seeks knowl- edge of the intelligibility to be found in our world. Whereas the other a priori disciplines (e.g., logic and mathematics) are concerned with intelligible relations that hold between abstract entities, philosophy is concerned with intelligible relations that hold between entities in the concrete spatiotemporal world in which we live.[5] I suggested earlier that we do not typically expect to find intelligibility in the world in which we live, but

philosophy embodies the perennial human hope that nevertheless we will find such intelligibility and succeed in articulating
it. We articulate the intelligibility of a thing when we articulate
what it is about that thing that enables there to be facts about
that thing that can be known a priori.

My characterization of philosophy will no doubt be a conten-
tious one, especially among philosophers themselves. Many philosophers throughout the centuries have objected to the view
that reason can discover things about the world in which we
live, a view standardly known as rationalism. I confess that I
have never been able to see what the problem is supposed to be
here. I know of no serious philosophical arguments that purport
to show that reason cannot discover things about the world; it is
difficult to conceive what such an argument would even look like
(wouldn't it itself have to be an argument produced by reason
purporting to tell us something about the world?). Regardless, I
am not interested in giving a full-fledged defense of rationalism
here; I hope a few brief remarks will suffice. First, I remind the
reader that the philosopher as I conceive him is not ignoring the
empirical facts; he is reflecting on these facts to discover further,
nonempirical facts. Thus, in the case of consciousness, my claim
is that as a result of introspection, we obtain knowledge of some
of the intrinsic properties of consciousness, and then by reflecting on these properties, we can obtain a priori knowledge of the
intelligible relations that hold among these properties. Certainly
it is a familiar idea that reason can detect (intelligible) relations
that hold between properties.[6]

The relations in question can be characterized as necessary
connections between distinct properties (existences), and many
philosophers object to the idea that there can be necessary
connections between distinct existences.[7] But this objection is

unfounded. Note as a preliminary point that the intelligible relations with which I am concerned indeed are necessary relations. When reason reflects on the intrinsic properties of consciousness with which introspection makes it familiar, what it is reflecting on is the essential nature of these properties, and when it discovers intelligible relations that hold among these properties, it is discovering relations that hold in virtue of the essential nature of these properties. So reason is discovering relations that *must* hold between these properties; it is discovering necessary relations. But I fail to see the objection to there being in the world necessary relations between distinct properties. The insistence that there *cannot* be such things just seems to be an unjustified a priori assumption about what the world can contain.

Ultimately my characterization of philosophy as the a priori discipline that seeks knowledge of the intelligible features of the world is to be defended in terms of its being the best description of what philosophers actually do. So let us remind ourselves of what philosophers do. Surely philosophers are not concerned merely with explicating our concepts; they are concerned with obtaining a priori knowledge of the world. This feature of philosophical activity is most salient in the area of philosophy known as metaphysics. Metaphysicians are concerned with finding intelligibility in the relations among the most general features of the world; they attempt to formulate accounts of these general features that will render intelligible the relations that hold among them. For example, they seek accounts of particulars and universals (and of instantiation) that render intelligible the idea of a particular instantiating a universal. It is no accident that metaphysics is often regarded as the core area of philosophy and that those who attack the legitimacy of philosophy commonly make metaphysics their special target. In metaphysics the essential nature of philosophy is made manifest. Nevertheless it is not difficult to see that philosophers in other areas of philosophy are also concerned with finding intelligibility in the world. Consider moral philosophy. Moral philosophers, at least those who recognize the existence of moral properties, are concerned with finding intelligible relations between moral properties and nonmoral (e.g., natural) properties. We all know that moral properties supervene on nonmoral properties; moral philosophers wish to exhibit the intelligibility of these supervenience relations. Similarly, epistemologists are looking for intelligible relations that hold between epistemic properties and nonepistemic properties; when they ask a question such as what makes a belief justified, they seek an answer that will articulate an intelligible relation between the property of being justified and the nonepistemic properties of a belief that make it justified. Philosophers of art seek intelligible relations between aesthetic properties and nonaesthetic properties. I leave it to the reader to provide further examples. Suffice it to say that even today, philosophers seem to be rationalists in practice if not in theory. For the most part, philosophers prefer to remain reticent about what they do and how they go about doing it; nevertheless, whether they admit it to themselves or not, most philosophers do seem to be employing their reason to find intelligibility in the world.

Finally, my characterization of philosophy has the virtue of explaining the difficulty of philosophy. It is not easy to find intelligibility in the world, and so philosophy is hard. Nevertheless philosophical inquiry begins when we at least suspect there to be some intelligibility in some part of the world. The task of philosophy is then to pin this intelligibility down, to specify the relevant intelligible relations and the properties that stand in them. Or perhaps we can identify the intelligible relation and even know that the relation is intelligible, but we need to engage in philosophical inquiry to determine what this intelligibility consists in or what makes the relation intelligible. Consider again the example of moral philosophy. We at least seem to know that moral properties supervene on nonmoral properties, and we suspect that the supervenience in question is intelligible, but we haven't yet succeeded in apprehending the nature of this intelligibility. We haven't yet specified what it is about the relations between moral properties and their subvening nonmoral properties that enables these relations to be known a priori. So the task of the moral philosopher is to specify the supervenience relations at issue (which moral properties supervene on which nonmoral properties) and to exhibit and articulate the intelligibility of these relations. Philosophical inquiry begins with partial grasps of intelligibility; such partial grasps are also forms of philosophical puzzlement. When the difficult work of philosophical inquiry succeeds and we find the intelligibility that we are looking for, our sense of puzzlement is removed, and we are left with pure, unadulterated wonder.

1.3   The Distraction of (Reductive) Physicalism

Philosophy seeks intelligibility in the world, and philosophy of mind should be no exception. There is intelligibility to be found in the realm of the mind, and philosophy of mind should focus on finding and articulating it. But, in fact, philosophy of mind has not typically focused on this task. I am not claiming that philosophers of mind have been looking for the intelligibility in the mind but for various reasons have not been able to find it; I am claiming that they have not even been looking for it. They have virtually ignored the essential philosophical task of finding the intelligibility characteristic of the mind.[8] Why have they ignored it? Because they have focused on other tasks, tasks that I regard as less important; they have been *distracted* from pursuing what should be their primary task. And at least in recent years, the cause of this distraction has been the unfortunate influence of the doctrine of physicalism.

Instead of focusing on the nature of the mind, philosophers of mind have generally focused on the nature of the relation between mind and body. Many philosophers have thought that the relation between mind and body seems at least to be problematic, and many of those philosophers have also thought that the only way to render the relation unproblematic is to hold that the properties of the mind are no different in kind from the properties of the body. The body, considered apart from the mind, is a physical object, and so bodily properties will be physical properties. The thought is that if the mind is to relate in an unproblematic way to the body, mental properties must be physical properties, also. Hence the popular philosophical idea that the solution to the mind–body problem is physicalism, the view that everything in the world, including the mind, is physical. (In section 1.4, I explain why I have not been persuaded by arguments for physicalism that purport to show that only physicalism can make sense of the relation between mind and body.)

But what exactly does it mean to characterize certain properties as *physical* properties? Paradigmatic physical objects are such things as tables, chairs, and rocks. An object is physical insofar as it has a physical nature. The nature of an object will be determined by the nature of its most basic parts. The basic parts of physical objects are the microscopic entities described by physics, so these microscopic entities can also be said to be physical.

Objects such as tables and chairs can then be said to be physical insofar as they are composed of these microscopic entities. And a *property* of a physical object is itself physical provided that its nature is somehow determined by the nature of these microscopic entities and the relations that hold between them.

Can we say more specifically what kinds of properties will count as physical properties? Physical properties will include *structural* properties. Structural physical properties are properties of being composed of certain specified physical entities (these being the microscopic entities referred to earlier) or of being composed of certain specified physical entities that stand in certain kinds of specified relations to each other. The physicalist view that holds that mental properties are identical to structural physical properties of the brain is the "identity" theory; it is most closely associated with J. J. C. Smart (1959). Physical properties can also be said to include the *causal* properties of physical objects that are realized by physical properties. A causal property is *realized* by some categorical (i.e., noncausal) property when an object has that causal property in virtue of having the underlying categorical property. Causal functionalism is the physicalist view that holds that mental properties are causal properties that are realized by physical properties; David Lewis (1966) and David Armstrong (1968) were early exponents. I will say that *reductive* physical properties are physical properties whose essential natures can be described without the use of mental terminology; reductive physical properties include structural physical properties, causal properties that are realized by physical properties, and perhaps other kinds of physical properties, also. And I will define *reductive physicalism* as the view that all mental properties are reductive physical properties. Reductive physicalism, which includes both the identity theory and causal functionalism,[9] has been the dominant position in the philosophy of mind since at least the middle of the last century.

Those who oppose reductive physicalism are *nonreductionists*; they hold that the essential natures of at least some mental properties cannot be described in nonmental terminology. I refer to these mental properties as *nonreductive* properties. These nonreductive mental properties cannot be described in nonmental terminology because they are sui generis; they are radically different from reductive physical properties, and with their appearance in the world something completely new begins to exist in the world. They are a new kind of basic, fundamental property. They are not complex structural physical properties or causal properties that are realized by physical properties; rather, they are simple, categorical properties. Nevertheless it is not part of the defining thesis of nonreductionism that these sui generis mental properties, which are not reductive physical properties, are not physical properties at all. Recall that what makes a property physical is that its nature is determined by the nature of those microscopic entities that constitute physical objects. So whether sui generis nonreductive mental properties are physical depends on whether their nature is determined by the nature of the aforementioned microscopic entities. Most philosophers of mind hold that their nature is not so determined, and therefore hold that nonreductive mental properties are not physical. Because most philosophers of mind hold this view, most nonreductionists are dualists, and most physicalists are reductive physicalists. In other words, most philosophers of mind who believe that nonreductive mental properties exist are (property) dualists, because they hold that these nonreductive mental properties are not physical. By contrast, most physicalists deny the existence of nonreductive mental properties (and are therefore reductive physicalists), because they, too, hold that nonreductive mental properties are not physical, and therefore their existence cannot be acknowledged by the physicalist.[10] But a few philosophers of mind hold that nonreductive mental properties exist, and also hold that these mental properties are physical. Such philosophers are nonreductive physicalists; they include Colin McGinn (1991), John Searle (1992), Galen Strawson (1994, 2008), and Thomas Nagel (2000). Nevertheless, as I noted earlier, the dominant position in the philosophy of mind is reductive physicalism, a position that denies the existence of nonreductive mental properties.

The guiding thesis of this book, that intelligibility is to be found in the mind, presupposes the truth of nonreductionism. As noted earlier (sec. 1.1), there is no intelligibility (in the relevant sense) to be found among nonmental phenomena; we cannot learn anything about the nonmental aspects of the physical world merely by reflecting on them. So if reductive physicalism is true and mental properties can be described in nonmental terminology, then we will not find intelligibility among mental phenomena, either. But I will show that we can find intelligibility among mental phenomena; specifically, when we reflect on some of the properties of consciousness, we can discover some of the relations that hold among these properties; these relations are thereby intelligible relations. By contrast, we cannot discover relations that hold among nonmental properties merely by reflecting on the nature of those properties. We can discover intelligibility in consciousness only because consciousness has an intrinsic nature that is fundamentally different from anything reductively physical, an intrinsic nature that can ground intelligible relations. The difference between consciousness and everything else is interesting and important only because it makes possible the intelligibility of the mind.

Given that the intelligibility of the mind presupposes nonreductionism, and given that reductive physicalism has been the dominant position in the philosophy of mind, it comes as no surprise that philosophers of mind have not succeeded in finding the intelligible features of the mind. For obvious reasons, reductive physicalists have not found these intelligible features. But nonreductionists have not found them either, for the dominance of reductive physicalism in the philosophy of mind has forced them to focus on things other than the search for intelligibility. Philosophers do not work in a vacuum; what they say is influenced by what other philosophers working on similar problems are saying. In particular, given that reductive physicalism is the dominant view in this area of philosophy, nonreductionists have in effect been forced to concentrate on "responding" to reductive physicalism instead of developing their own nonreductionist view of the mind. Instead of describing and elucidating the intelligible relations that hold among the properties of consciousness, nonreductionists spend virtually all their time arguing for the nonreductionist thesis that there are nonreductive mental properties, and responding to arguments for the reductive physicalist thesis that all mental properties are reductive physical properties. They spend so much time defending the basic nonreductionist thesis that they have no time to develop this thesis into a full-fledged theory of the mind. Because of the dominance of reductive physicalism in the philosophy of mind, philosophy of mind is dominated by a back-and-forth between the nonreductionist and the reductive physicalist that not only fails to shed any light on the nature of the mind but also prevents philosophers of mind from doing the work that they should be doing—finding and articulating the intelligible features of the mind. Reductive physicalism has set the agenda in the philosophy of mind and in so doing has had an unfortunate influence on both its practitioners and its opponents.

I do not want reductive physicalists to set my agenda, so I will not allow them to do so. Instead I devote the bulk of this book to articulating some of the intelligible features of consciousness and to describing their relevance to certain other important features of the mind. I spend little time arguing for nonreductionism or responding to arguments for (reductive) physicalism. In short, for the most part, I ignore physicalism. Perhaps there is some concern that if I proceed in this manner, I will be acting in a philosophically irresponsible manner; I will be begging the philosophical question in favor of nonreductionism. But I argue that the question that divides nonreductionism from reductive physicalism is not a philosophical question and therefore cannot be resolved by philosophical argument. I am not acting in a philosophically irresponsible manner by ignoring physicalism, as I argue in the following section.

1.4 How to Ignore Physicalism

My aim is to articulate some of the intelligible features of consciousness. As I noted in the previous section, if consciousness has intelligible features, then nonreductionism must be true, for intelligible relations can hold among the properties of consciousness only if there are nonreductive properties of consciousness to ground these intelligible relations (reductive physical properties do not ground intelligible relations). Therefore I am a nonreductionist. But unlike most nonreductionists who write about the nature of the mind, I am not preoccupied with presenting arguments for nonreductionism, responding to arguments for (reductive) physicalism, or finding flaws with particular reductive physicalist accounts of the mind. How do I justify this refusal to engage with the physicalist?

I do not argue for nonreductionism because my knowledge of nonreductionism is not based on argument; it is based on introspection. As human beings, we believe ourselves to be able to obtain knowledge of the world through having a kind of direct contact with it; this kind of direct contact is referred to as observation. When we have such direct contact with the world, we can obtain knowledge of that portion of the world with which we have contact. When one has contact with portions of the world external to one's mind, we talk of perception; when one has contact with portions of one's own mind, we speak of introspection. I take myself to have learned through introspection that the mind has properties that are not reductive physical properties: it has properties that are neither structural nor causal properties.

When we learn about the world through contact with it, we are said to have (empirical) evidence for what we learn. I don't need an a priori philosophical argument for nonreductionism, for I have empirical introspective evidence that nonreductionism is true. It is sometimes suggested that there is something intellectually disreputable about nonreductionism (or about its close cousin, dualism). But surely an important principle of responsible intellectual inquiry is to take one's evidence seriously. It is the nonreductionist who takes his introspective evidence seriously, while the reductive physicalist ignores or cavalierly dismisses the evidence about the nature of mental properties.

But haven't I said that the description of the intelligible features of consciousness is a task for philosophy, a task that requires the employment of reason? We need to be clear about the division of labor here. It is introspection that informs us of the existence and nature of nonreductive properties of consciousness; by employing our reason to reflect on these properties, we discover intelligible relations that hold among these properties. As noted earlier (sec. 1.2), although philosophy is an a priori discipline, it does not ignore familiar empirical facts; rather, it reflects on them. And among the familiar empirical facts we need to obtain a priori knowledge of the intelligible features of consciousness is the familiar fact of nonreductionism.

Some will insist that I have gone too far in describing nonreductionism as a familiar empirical fact. But surely we do take nonreductionism to be a familiar fact. For although reductive physicalism is the dominant view in the philosophy of mind, dualism, the most familiar form of nonreductionism, is the commonsense view. Nonreductionism is the view that there are mental properties that are not reductive physical properties; in other words, there are mental properties that are neither structural physical properties nor causal properties that are realized by physical properties. In other words, mind is different from body. But everyone agrees that mind at least *seems* to be something different from body. It is because mind seems to be different from body that many have thought there to be a mind–body problem, a problem about how mind is related to body. The reductive physicalist solves this apparent problem by identifying mental properties with reductive physical properties. If mental properties are just reductive physical properties, then there is no problem as to how mental and bodily properties are related. But then presumably the physicalist acknowledges that there at least seems to be a mind–body problem, or else he would not identify mental properties with reductive physical properties in an attempt to solve the apparent problem. There seems to be a mind–body problem, for mental properties seem to be something other than reductive physical properties. In other words, nonreductionism seems to us to be true, and it seems to us to be true because we take ourselves to have introspective evidence for its truth.[11]

The reductive physicalist ignores our introspective evidence for nonreductionism, and one cannot have a fruitful discussion with someone who refuses to acknowledge relevant evidence. I take nonreductionism to be true because I take myself to have introspected nonreductive mental properties; if the reductive physicalist insists on denying that he can introspect such properties, there is nothing I can say that will persuade him otherwise. Surely I will be unable to persuade him of the truth of nonreductionism by *argument*. Nonreductionism is such a plausible thesis because we seem to have introspective evidence for it. The reductive physicalist who is willing to deny this very plausible thesis will have no compunctions about denying premises in an argument for this very plausible thesis. Such premises will be no more plausible than the nonreductionist thesis itself.

A good many arguments for nonreductionism are put forth in the contemporary philosophical literature (many of these are presented as arguments for dualism),[12] but such arguments are misleading in that they misrepresent the nature of our knowledge of nonreductionism. Our knowledge of nonreductionism is based on empirical introspection, not a priori philosophical argument. Whether nonreductive mental properties exist in the world is something to be determined by investigating the world, not by thinking about it. It will not do to say that introspection tells us that we instantiate mental properties but that conceptual analysis is needed to tell us that our concepts of these properties are concepts of nonreductive properties. I acknowledge that we possess concepts of nonreductive mental properties, but we possess these concepts because we introspected nonreductive mental properties and then formed concepts of them. Introspection does not inform us merely that we instantiate mental properties; it informs us of the nature of these properties, and we thereby realize that their nature is nonreductive: it cannot be described with nonmental terminology. Introspection is doing all the work in informing us of the truth of nonreductionism; any philosophical argumentation is otiose.

Consider the arguments for nonreductionism to be found in the contemporary literature. The premises of all these arguments cite various *modal* features of mental properties. They make various claims about ways it is *possible* for mental properties to exist or fail to exist in relation to reductive physical properties, or ways it is possible for our knowledge of mental properties to relate to our knowledge of reductive physical properties. From these premises about modal features of mental properties, we are supposed to reach a conclusion about an *actual* feature of mental properties—that they are actually not identical to reductive physical properties. Saul Kripke, for example, argues as follows against the identity theory: given any structural physical property of the brain, it is possible for a subject to feel pain in the absence of that structural physical property being instantiated, and therefore the property of feeling pain is not in fact identical to any structural physical property of the brain (1980, lecture 3). The suggestion seems to be that we begin with a priori insight into modal features of mental properties, and on the basis of that insight we obtain knowledge of an actual feature of mental properties, that they are not identical to structural physical properties of the brain. But this gets things backward. In fact, I claim, we begin with knowledge of the nature of (some) mental properties, knowledge we obtain by introspection, and on the basis of that knowledge, we obtain knowledge of various modal features of mental properties. Again, it is introspection that informs us of the nature of mental properties, not a priori reflection.[13]

Perhaps the reductive physicalist will counter that he is not ignoring the introspective evidence for nonreductionism but believes that such evidence can be somehow outweighed or neutralized by the arguments for reductive physicalism. But how such outweighing is supposed to work is not clear. We do not merely have evidence for the truth of nonreductionism; we have direct evidence. Nonreductionism is not a theoretical claim that can be supported by empirical evidence only with the assistance of some kind of inductive, explanatory, or probabilistic reasoning; rather, nonreductionism is an observational claim. It is the thesis that some mental properties are nonreductive, and that thesis is what I am informed of by introspection. Specifically, introspection informs me of the intrinsic nature of mental properties; it informs me that there are mental properties that are simple and categorical and thus nonreductive. Given this direct connection between nonreductionism and the evidence that supports it, it is unclear how this evidence can be outweighed (or neutralized, undermined, or defeated) by philosophical arguments for reductive physicalism. Such arguments inevitably appeal to theoretical considerations that do not enjoy the kind of direct evidential support enjoyed by nonreductionism. Therefore the proper response to such an argument will always be to deny one of its premises, for such an argument will always contain a premise that has weaker evidential support than the nonreductionist thesis itself.

In sum, I do not need to engage in a detailed examination of the arguments for reductive physicalism, because I know in advance that I can with justification reject each such argument, for each such argument will contain at least one premise less plausible than the nonreductionist thesis itself. Consider, for example, the following standard argument for (reductive) physicalism:

(1) Conscious mental occurrences have physical effects.

(2) All physical effects have sufficient physical causes.

(3) The physical effects of conscious causes are not always overdetermined.

Therefore:

The conscious occurrences mentioned in (1) are identical to (parts of) the physical causes mentioned in (2).[14]

I am sympathetic with (1), and so I will focus on how a nonreductionist can challenge (2) or (3). I submit that no matter how plausible you think (2) and (3) are, they are surely less plausible than the nonreductionist thesis itself. The nonreductionist thesis has direct evidential support, where (2) and (3) have, at most, inductive evidential support. The claim in (2) is a theoretical claim about *all* (reductive) physical effects; it is theoretical in that it applies to unobservable physical effects as well as observable ones, and the sufficient (reductive) physical causes it mentions include unobservable causes, also. We do not have direct evidential support for (2) because we have not observed the truth of (2), for we have not observed all physical effects. When we do observe physical effects, we often do not observe their sufficient causes. The evidential support for (3) is even weaker, for we do seem to observe cases of causal overdetermination.[15] By contrast, consider the evidence for nonreductionism: when I am awake, I continuously have conscious states, and whenever I have a conscious state, I can observe the nonreductive nature of that state. I conclude that anyone who takes evidence seriously will not be persuaded by arguments for reductive physicalism and so can safely ignore them.

Of course, evidence is sometimes misleading. The moon appears to me to be small, but it isn't, so perhaps mental properties only appear to me to have a nonreductive nature, but in fact they don't. In other words, perhaps introspection is infected by a pervasive illusion.[16] Or perhaps my belief in nonreductionism is not the product of introspection at all. Perhaps it only seems to me that I am observing my mind, and in fact I am not. Or perhaps it only seems to me that introspection informs me of the nature of mental properties, when it fact it doesn't.[17] In other words, perhaps the commonsense belief in dualist nonreductionism is the product of something akin to a collective introspective hallucination. Perhaps. But other things being equal, we take our evidence at face value, and so we should ignore a physicalist who groundlessly impugns our introspective evidence. Of course, instead of merely raising the possibility that our introspective evidence is misleading, a physicalist is free to *argue* that our introspective evidence for nonreductionism is in fact the product of illusion or hallucination. I am doubtful that the physicalist will be able to come up with a persuasive argument here, an argument all of whose premises are more plausible than the nonreductionist thesis itself. But I am open-minded; if the physicalist purports to have a persuasive argument that the best explanation for our putative evidence for nonreductionism is that it is a product of introspective illusion or hallucination, then I will listen to him.[18] Meanwhile I will not waste any more time defending nonreductionism; rather, I will take my introspective evidence for nonreductionism at face value and reflect on it in an attempt to find and articulate the intelligible features of consciousness.

Nonetheless I should note that there is a sense in which this book can be understood as a philosophical argument for nonreductionism. As I noted earlier (sec. 1.1), I am arguing that adequate accounts of rationality, knowledge, and the role of value in our lives must advert to the intelligibility of consciousness. But the intelligibility of consciousness presupposes nonreductionism (sec. 1.3). Therefore, insofar as I succeed in the argument of this book, I will also have succeeded in arguing for nonreductionism. I would therefore ask even those readers who would reject out of hand the idea that we have introspective evidence for nonreductionism to keep an open mind and to continue reading with the aim of discovering what philosophical feats we might accomplish on the assumption that we do have introspective evidence for nonreductionism.

1.5   The Intelligibility of Consciousness: A First Step

I do not purport here to describe all the intelligible features of consciousness. The intelligible features of consciousness are naturally thought of as intelligible features of conscious states. There is a wide variety of different kinds of conscious states, and presumably different kinds of conscious states will have different kinds of intelligible features. Among the different kinds of conscious states are perceptual experiences, bodily sensations, feelings, judgments, decisions, acts of imagining, and acts of willing. There are also mental states such as emotions, memories, thoughts, beliefs, desires, and intentions that seem to occur in both conscious and unconscious forms. I will not be discussing all these different kinds of conscious states, primarily because I do not at present know and understand all their intelligible features. I will focus on mental states such as perceptual experiences, beliefs, bodily sensations, feelings, and desires. I will especially be focusing on the intelligible features of (perceptual) experiences.

My first task, then, is to describe the intelligible features of experiences. Note that I am not claiming to have *discovered* that intelligible features are to be found in consciousness; I mean only to specify and articulate the nature of intelligible features with which we are already, in some sense, familiar. I think that the wonder of consciousness is obvious to everyone. But what is wonderful about consciousness is its intelligibility, so I am claiming that the intelligibility of consciousness is obvious to everyone. We all know that consciousness is intelligible; what is difficult is articulating the nature of this intelligibility. Philosophical inquiry begins with partial grasps of intelligibility (sec. 1.2); thus I begin my inquiry with this partial grasp we all have of the intelligibility of perceptual experience.

I am not saying that people go around explicitly describing various features of experience as intelligible. I am saying that we commonly describe experience in ways that seem to imply that intelligibility is to be found in experience. John McDowell has nicely captured some of these familiar ways of describing experience. Thus we say that in experience, the world reveals itself to us or "makes itself manifest" to us (McDowell 1994, 39). The world can reveal itself to us in experience because experience involves "an openness to the layout of reality" (26); therefore "in experience one can take in how things are" (25). Some would be inclined to dismiss such descriptions as metaphorical; McDowell himself refers here to the "image of openness to reality" (26). But we resort to imagistic language here precisely because we sense intelligibility but cannot describe its nature literally. In fact, McDowell's language points to at least two kinds of intelligible relations to be found in experience.

If talk of the world revealing itself to us in experience is to be appropriate, then an intelligible relation must obtain between the world and experience. More specifically, an intelligible relation must obtain between the intrinsic nature of an experience and the portion of the world that is revealed in the experience, the portion of the world that the experience is an experience *of*. We can also put the point in terms of consciousness; there must be an intelligible relation between the "conscious" quality of an experience and the portion of the world that the subject is conscious of in having the experience. A mere brute causal connection between the world and experience is insufficient, for if the world really *reveals* itself to us in experience, then if we reflect on an experience, we should be able to find the world there. In other words, the relation between experience and the world should be detectable by reason. But a relation that is detectable by reason is an intelligible relation (sec. 1.1). So when we talk of the world revealing itself to us in experience, we are committed to there being intelligible relations between experiences and the world.

Of course there is something puzzling about the idea of an intelligible relation between experience and the world. I believe in the truth of nonreductionism (sec. 1.4): mental properties are different from nonmental properties, and so experiences of the world are different from the world that is experienced. It may seem puzzling that two such different things can be related in an intelligible way, in a way that can be detected by reason. In chapter 2, I attempt to articulate the nature of this intelligible relation in a way that removes our sense of puzzlement.

Not only does an intelligible relation obtain between experience and the world, but an intelligible relation also obtains between experience and our knowledge of the world. Surely, if the world reveals itself to us in experience, then we can obtain knowledge of the world as the result of experiencing it. The idea that experience gives rise to knowledge is a familiar one. But what I am claiming here is not merely that experience gives rise to knowledge but that, given the nature of experience (as revealing the world to us), it *makes sense* by the lights of reason that it should give rise to knowledge; in other words, that experience gives rise to knowledge is an intelligible fact. Knowledge is at least true belief, so insofar as it is intelligible that experiences give rise to knowledge, it will be intelligible that experiences can cause certain kinds of true beliefs. In other words, an intelligible relation will obtain between certain of an experience's causal powers (its powers to produce certain kinds of true beliefs) and the intrinsic properties that ground those causal powers. In chapter 3, I explain the nature of this intelligible relation.

2 The Intelligibility of Consciousness I: How Experience Relates Us to the World

2.1 The Intrinsic Nature of Experience

In this chapter, I focus on some of the intelligible features of (perceptual) experiences. As I indicated earlier (sec. 1.2), we can discover the intelligible features of conscious states by reflecting on the familiar intrinsic properties of conscious states made known to us through introspection. So let us begin by considering the familiar intrinsic properties of experience.

An experience is the event of a subject instantiating a certain kind of mental property, and a subject can introspect this property when he has the experience. The introspectible properties that define experiences are typically referred to in the contemporary literature as *phenomenal* properties; philosophers also speak of the *phenomenal character* of an experience. Now the word "phenomenal" is just a word, and so there can be no harm in using it to refer to the properties in question. Nevertheless, when we employ the term "phenomenal" to refer to these properties, we need to take care not to be misled. Philosophers talk of phenomenal character as the property of an experience, not of an *experiencer*. But as I noted, phenomenal properties are, in the first instance, properties of experiencers, of *subjects* of experience; the occurrence of an experience just is the event of a subject instantiating a certain kind of mental property. So although, in conformity with current usage, I talk of phenomenal character and phenomenal properties as properties of experiences, we need to keep in mind that these properties are in fact properties of subjects of experience, properties whose instantiation by a subject constitutes the subject's experience. (Of course there is nothing wrong with thinking of phenomenal properties as properties of experiences in some derivative sense.)

Thomas Nagel's famous "what it is like" terminology is in fact more precise here, for what-it-is-like properties are clearly properties of experiencers, not experiences. According to Nagel, "an organism has conscious mental states if and only if there is something that it is like to *be* that organism—something it is like *for* the organism" (1974, 436; italics in original). To say that there is something it is like for the organism to be that organism is surely to ascribe a property to the organism, and to say *what* it is like for the organism to be that organism is to ascribe a more determinate property to the organism. The experiential properties that I am concerned with here are a subset of Nagel's what-it-is-like properties; they are only a subset of these properties because a subject has what-it-is-like properties whenever he has any kind of conscious mental state, but we are concerned for now only with the what-it-is-like properties associated with perceptual experiences.

So what does introspection tell us about the intrinsic nature of these what-it-is-like properties, or, less awkwardly, what does introspection tell us about the nature of phenomenal properties? (I use "phenomenal properties" and "what-it-is-like properties" as synonyms.) It is difficult to say anything specific about the distinctive intrinsic nature of phenomenal properties, and some physicalists would thereby conclude that introspection does not in fact inform us of the nature of phenomenal properties.[1] But such a conclusion would be too hasty. We might have knowledge of the nature of a property without being able to describe it. The nature of the property might be such that it *cannot* be described; its nature might be *simple*, so to speak. Consider the example of colors. Consider, more specifically, the sensory natures of colors, as opposed to, say, the microstructural properties that underlie them. We cannot describe the intrinsic sensory natures of red, blue, brown, or any of the other colors, for such sensory natures are simple.[2] Nevertheless there is surely a sense in which we know their natures. (Look at a red tomato. Look at that color spread out on the surface of the tomato. *That* is the sensory nature of redness.) And perhaps something similar is true for the intrinsic nature of phenomenal properties. Perhaps we can know what it is like to experience the redness of an object without being able to describe it.

Some will be suspicious of the idea that there can be such inexpressible knowledge. But I intend the example of our knowledge of colors to disabuse us of this suspicion. Our observation of the world, whether in the form of perception or introspection, does not merely inform us that certain objects have certain properties; it tells us something about these properties. (If it did not tell us something about these properties, it is not clear how it could inform us that objects had these properties.) If the properties in question are simple, then our knowledge of their nature will be inexpressible. Some will insist that any knowledge deserving of the name must be propositional knowledge, knowledge *that* something is the case, and that inexpressible knowledge of the nature of a property is not propositional knowledge and therefore is not really knowledge at all. I wish to remain neutral on the questions of whether all knowledge should be understood as propositional knowledge or even whether inexpressible knowledge of a property should, in a final theoretical accounting, be understood as propositional knowledge. Regardless, at an intuitive level it certainly seems reasonable to think of inexpressible knowledge of a property as a kind of propositional knowledge. My knowledge of the (sensory) nature of redness is propositional knowledge that the nature of redness is *that*, and my knowledge of the nature of what it is like to experience redness is propositional knowledge that what it is like to experience redness is *that*. Observation of the world relates both sensory and phenomenal properties to our minds in a way that enables us to refer to them demonstratively and thereby to have propositional knowledge of their nature.

Even if it is granted that we can have knowledge of the intrinsic natures of phenomenal properties without being able to describe them, one might still question the interest or usefulness of this knowledge. What is the point of knowing the nature of a phenomenal property if I can't articulate it? The point of this knowledge is that it gives rise to further knowledge of the properties of experience, knowledge that can be articulated. The most obvious instance is that in virtue of knowing the nature of phenomenal properties, I know that phenomenal properties are neither structural properties nor causal properties; in other words, I know the truth of nonreductionism (sec. 1.4). I know this precisely because the natures of phenomenal properties are such that they cannot be straightforwardly described, whereas the natures of structural and causal properties are such that they can be straightforwardly described. Causal properties include properties of being "apt to be the cause of certain effects" and properties of being "apt to be the effect of certain causes" (Armstrong 1980,

20); one describes these properties by specifying the relevant effects and causes. Structural properties are described by specifying the relevant structures. I know that phenomenal properties are not structural properties or causal properties because I know that the nature of phenomenal properties cannot be described in the ways that structural and causal properties are described. The point is not that I fail to detect structure or causal function and therefore (mistakenly, according to the reductive physicalist) assume that phenomenal properties are not structural or causal properties.[3] The point is that I have positive knowledge that what it is like to experience red is *that*, and I also know that *that* is not a structure or causal function. In virtue of having inexpressible knowledge of what phenomenal properties are, we are able to have and express our knowledge of what phenomenal properties are not.

But our inexpressible knowledge of what phenomenal properties are does not give rise merely to expressible knowledge of what phenomenal properties are not; it also gives rise to further positive knowledge about phenomenal properties and experiences, positive knowledge that *is* expressible. Recall that the underlying idea of this philosophical inquiry is that we can discover the intelligible features of consciousness by reflecting on the intrinsic features of consciousness made known to us through introspection. Specifically, not only does introspection enable us to refer demonstratively to phenomenal properties and thereby to have knowledge of their nature; it also enables us to reflect on their nature, with the result that we discover further features of phenomenal properties and the experiences that have them. These further features can be discovered by reflection on the nature of phenomenal properties because they are intelligibly related to the nature of phenomenal properties (sec.

1.1). Given that phenomenal properties have the nature that they do, they (or the corresponding experiences) *must* have certain further properties, and it is intelligible that they do so. They have these further properties *in virtue of* having the nature that they do. Thus the real significance of our inexpressible knowledge of the nature of phenomenal properties is that it enables us to gain knowledge of the intelligible features of experiences.

To see how this works, consider, again, the example of colors. As noted earlier, we have inexpressible knowledge of the intrinsic sensory natures of various colors. By reflecting on these sensory natures, we gain *expressible* knowledge about colors. We gain knowledge, say, of the similarity and difference relations that hold among the colors. For instance, I know that red is more similar to orange than it is to blue. This relation is an intelligible relation (sec. 1.1): given the natures of red, orange, and blue, it is intelligible that they should be related in this way, and therefore reason can discover this relation by reflecting on their natures. Red is more similar to orange than it is to blue *in virtue of* the sensory natures of red, orange, and blue. So not only does our knowledge of the intrinsic sensory natures of the colors enable us to discover the intelligible similarity and difference relations that hold among the colors; it also enables us to understand why these relations hold, for through reflection we are able to see how these similarity and difference relations are intelligibly connected to the natures of the colors.

What is true for colors is also true for phenomenal properties: by reflecting on the natures of phenomenal properties, we can discover and understand their intelligible features. Moreover, just as there are intelligible similarity relations that hold among the colors, so too there are corresponding intelligible similarity relations that hold among the corresponding phenomenal properties. What it is like to experience the redness of an object is more similar to what it is like to experience orange than it is to what it is like to experience blue. Let us use terms such as *phenomenal red*, *phenomenal orange*, and *phenomenal blue* to refer to the aforementioned phenomenal properties (i.e., what-it-is-like properties). So we can say more concisely that phenomenal red is more similar to phenomenal orange than it is to phenomenal blue. This relation holds in virtue of the natures of the relevant phenomenal properties and can be discovered by reflecting on their nature.

Now, although the similarity relations holding among phenomenal properties are indeed intelligible relations, they are not interesting intelligible relations. We are interested in getting at what makes consciousness distinctive, what makes it different from everything else in the world. But as we have seen, the similarity relations that hold among phenomenal properties are shared by the corresponding sensory properties (i.e., colors, sounds, smells, etc.), and so they don't distinguish phenomenal properties from sensory properties. Nevertheless this parallel between phenomenal properties and sensory properties points us in the right direction if we want to get at what is distinctive about consciousness. Surely it is no accident that phenomenal properties and sensory properties stand in identical similarity (and difference) relations.

Perhaps some will be inclined to explain this parallel by identifying phenomenal properties with sensory properties. But a few moments of reflection will show that such identification is a mistake. Not only are phenomenal properties not identical to structural or causal properties, but they are not identical to sensory properties, either.[4] It is one thing for a physical object or even a mental object such as an afterimage to have the sensory property of being red; it is quite another for a *subject* to be *experiencing* that sensory property and for there to be something it is like for the subject to be experiencing that property. Suppose, again, that you are looking at a red tomato. The sensory redness you are looking at is spread out in space on the surface of the tomato; it is a property of the tomato and is located where the tomato is located. But what it is like for you to be looking at that redness is not a property of the tomato; it is a phenomenal property that *you* are instantiating, and if located anywhere, it is located where you are located. Moreover, even if the instantiation of the phenomenal property can be located in space, it is not spread out in the space in which you are located in the way the sensory redness is spread out over the surface of the tomato. You are looking at sensory redness spread out in space, but what it is like for you to be doing so is not itself spread out in space. Clearly the sensory redness we experience is not identical to the phenomenal redness that constitutes such experience.

It is perception that informs us of the nature of observable properties such as (sensory) colors, and it is introspection that informs us of the nature of phenomenal properties such as phenomenal colors. Reflection on the natures of the colors informs us of the similarity relations that hold among the colors, and reflection on the natures of the phenomenal colors informs us of the similarity relations that hold among the phenomenal colors. Now, even those who are willing to accept my argument that phenomenal properties are distinct from sensory properties may be suspicious of my claim that we have knowledge of two sets of similarity relations here. But perhaps the problem is that people do not typically introspect their phenomenal properties, and therefore many people do not have knowledge of the similarity relations that hold among the phenomenal colors. We

perceive colors whenever we open our eyes, but we do not introspect phenomenal colors unless we make some special effort to
do so. When we open our eyes, we have visual perceptual experiences and thereby perceive colors, but though these perceptual
experiences have phenomenal properties, we do not introspect
these phenomenal properties merely in virtue of having the
experiences; we have to do the extra work of introspecting them.
Generally we have no reason to do this extra work, for in everyday life we typically have no reason to introspect phenomenal
properties. (Moreover, it is somewhat difficult to introspect phenomenal properties, as I explain in section 6 of chapter 3.) So it
should not be surprising that some people think that they do
not have knowledge of phenomenal properties that are distinct
from sensory properties, or some think that they do not have
knowledge of similarity relations holding among phenomenal
properties that is distinct from their knowledge of the similarity
relations holding among sensory properties. Nevertheless, even
if some of us do not have such knowledge, we can obtain it: we
can introspect our phenomenal properties, and we can obtain
knowledge of the similarity relations that hold among them.

But if phenomenal properties are not identical to sensory properties, then how do we explain the fact, noted a few paragraphs
earlier, that phenomenal properties and sensory properties share
their similarity relations? Presumably it is because phenomenal
properties are similar to their corresponding sensory properties,
even though they are not identical to them. Reflection on both
sensory and phenomenal properties informs us of the similarity
relations that hold between them. There is a kind of similarity
between redness and what it is like to experience redness. Also,
what it is like to experience blue is similar to blue, what it is like
to experience sweetness is similar to sweetness, and even what

it is like to experience squareness, say, is similar to squareness. The similarities hold not only between phenomenal properties and sensory properties but more generally between phenomenal properties and (perceptually) observable properties (spatial properties are nonsensory but observable). As we will see, it is because of these similarities *between* phenomenal properties and observable properties that the similarities *among* phenomenal properties correspond to the similarities among the corresponding observable properties. For example, it is because of the similarities between phenomenal red and red, phenomenal orange and orange, and phenomenal blue and blue that phenomenal red is more similar to phenomenal orange than it is to phenomenal blue, just as red is more similar to orange than it is to blue.

The similarities between phenomenal properties and corresponding observable properties are intelligible similarities. Given the intrinsic natures of redness and phenomenal redness, say, it is an intelligible fact that a certain kind of similarity holds between them, and therefore reason can discover this similarity by reflecting on their natures. If we wish to understand what makes consciousness distinctive, we need to understand the nature of this intelligible similarity.

2.2 The Intelligible Relations between Observable Properties and Phenomenal Properties

Consider, again, the intelligible similarity between phenomenal redness and redness. Similarity is a symmetric relation; phenomenal redness is similar to redness, and redness is similar to phenomenal redness. But reflection on the intrinsic natures of phenomenal redness and redness reveals that what accounts for the intelligible similarity between them is an intelligible asymmetric relation between them. The intrinsic nature of phenomenal properties cannot be described, and so phenomenal properties cannot be structural properties, because structural properties can be described. Nevertheless, as I explain hereafter, reflection reveals that phenomenal properties are something like structural properties, and their corresponding observable properties are something like elements of the associated (quasi-)structures. In brief, the relation between a phenomenal property and a corresponding observable property is something like the (intelligible) relation between whole and part.

How is the relation between phenomenal property and corresponding observable property similar to the relation between whole and part? The relation between part and whole is, among other things, an explanatory relation: the nature of the part provides a partial explanation of the nature of the whole of which it is a part. Moreover, assuming that the whole is not more than the sum of its parts, the explanatory relation in question will be an intelligible explanatory relation, for mere reflection on the natures of the whole and the part will reveal how the nature of the part contributes to the nature of the whole. What I wish to claim here is that the relation between observable property and phenomenal property is also an intelligible explanatory relation; mere reflection on the intrinsic natures of an observational property and its corresponding phenomenal property reveals that the nature of the observable property (partly) explains why the nature of the phenomenal property is the way it is. The nature of red, for example, partly explains the nature of what it is like to experience red. And the way that an observable property intelligibly and partly explains its corresponding phenomenal property is something like the way in which a part intelligibly and partly explains the whole of which it is a part.

Note that not all explanatory relations are intelligible relations. Causal relations are explanatory relations, but most philosophers follow David Hume in holding that causal relations are not intelligible relations. According to Hume, causal relations cannot be known a priori: mere reflection on the intrinsic nature of an event will not reveal its causal powers. Similarly, according to Hume, mere reflection on the intrinsic nature of two events that are in fact related as cause and effect will not reveal that they are related as cause and effect; empirical investigation is needed to discover what causes what in the world.[5] But the part–whole relation and the observable property–phenomenal property relation are intelligible explanatory relations. We need no empirical investigation to discover how an observable property explains its corresponding phenomenal property; mere reflection on their natures is sufficient.

Insofar as the explanatory relation between observable property and phenomenal property can be discovered by reflection on the (essential) natures of these properties, the explanatory relation will not only be intelligible but will also be a necessary relation. Given the natures of redness and phenomenal redness, say, it is necessary that a certain kind of explanatory relation exist between them. We can also make this point by saying that given the nature of redness, it is necessary that the phenomenal property explained by redness be phenomenal redness. Redness *necessitates* the nature of phenomenal redness; if it did not, it could not intelligibly explain its nature. But I submit that the necessity also goes in the opposite direction. Given the nature of phenomenal redness, it is necessary that the observable property that explains its nature be redness. Not all explanatory relations are necessary in both directions; causes necessitate their effects, but effects don't necessitate their causes, for two different causes can have the same effect. But only one observable property can explain the nature of phenomenal redness: redness itself. So mere reflection on the nature of phenomenal redness informs us of the nature of the observable property that explains the nature of phenomenal redness. In other words, an experience of red reveals to us the presence of redness in the world.

Insofar as redness explains and necessitates the nature of phenomenal redness, redness can be said to *determine* phenomenal redness. More generally, I am claiming that observable properties determine phenomenal properties. Philosophers of mind dispute exactly what determines the phenomenal properties of an experience. *Representationalists* (also known as *intentionalists*) hold that the phenomenal character of an experience is determined (solely) by its representational properties, whereas qualia theorists hold that the phenomenal character of an experience is determined (at least in part) by certain of its nonrepresentational properties, properties that are standardly referred to as *qualia*.[6] So, for example, consider an experience of a red object. The representationalist holds that the phenomenal redness of the experience is determined by the experience's property of representing the object as red, whereas the qualia theorist holds that it is determined by the experience's red qualia. My position is that the phenomenal redness is determined by the actual redness of the experienced physical object. How does my position relate to the positions of the representationalist and qualia theorist? I am probably best understood here as being a kind of qualia theorist. Qualia theorists seem to hold that qualia are sensory properties, and I too hold that the properties that determine the phenomenal properties of color experiences (phenomenal colors) are sensory properties.[7] The only difference between us is that I hold these sensory properties to be the colors, whereas the qualia theorist characterizes them as color qualia. But for purposes of getting clear about the properties that determine the phenomenal colors, we can ignore this difference. The qualia theorist and I agree about which properties determine the phenomenal colors; we only disagree about what to call them, "colors" or "color qualia." We also seem to disagree about whether these sensory properties are properties of the physical objects we experience (my view) or properties of the experiences themselves (the qualia theorist's view). But there is a sense in which I can accept the view of the qualia theorist that these sensory properties are properties of experiences. As I explain in the following section, my view is a direct realist one according to which the object one experiences is literally a part of one's experience.[8] (This is not idealism; the physical object is part of the experience while the experience is occurring, but the physical object continues to exist even when it is not experienced.) So if the sensory properties that determine phenomenal colors are properties of experienced physical objects, then in a derivative sense they are properties of experiences, as well. I have already suggested that an observable property relates to its corresponding phenomenal property in a way similar to the way in which a part relates to its whole. In line with this idea, I am now suggesting that the objects that have these observable properties are parts of the experiences that have these phenomenal properties.

I do not wish to suggest that there are no substantive differences between my view and the view of the typical qualia theorist. Whereas I hold that phenomenal colors, say, are determined by corresponding properties of experienced physical objects (the colors), the qualia theorist holds that phenomenal colors are *not* determined by properties of experienced physical objects; they are determined by properties of experiences. The qualia theorist would presumably appeal here to the existence of hallucinations and illusions. Not only veridical perceptual experiences have phenomenal properties; illusions and hallucinations have them, also. I agree with the qualia theorist that phenomenal colors are determined by (instantiations of) corresponding sensory properties. So the phenomenal colors of color illusions and hallucinations will be determined by corresponding sensory properties, as well. But in the cases of illusions and hallucinations, argues the qualia theorist, the needed sensory properties are not instantiated in experienced physical objects. In the case of hallucinations, no physical objects are experienced at all. In the case of an illusion, the experienced physical object appears to have a color that it does not have, but it is the color that the physical object appears to have that is needed to determine the phenomenal color of the illusory experience. So the sensory properties that determine the phenomenal colors of illusions and hallucinations cannot be properties of experienced physical objects; they must be properties of the experiences themselves. But presumably, argues the qualia theorist, the sensory properties that determine the phenomenal colors of veridical experiences must be of the same type as the sensory properties that determine the phenomenal colors of illusions and hallucinations. So if the sensory properties that determine the phenomenal colors of illusions and hallucinations are not properties of experienced physical objects, then the sensory properties that determine the phenomenal colors of veridical experiences are not properties of experienced physical objects, either. They also are properties of experiences; in other words, they are color qualia.[9]

In response to this argument, I acknowledge that the sensory colors that determine the phenomenal colors of hallucinations are not properties of experienced physical objects, but I maintain that the sensory colors that determine the phenomenal colors of nonhallucinatory experiences *are* properties of experienced physical objects. In other words, I adopt a version of what has become known as *disjunctivism*: the observable properties that determine the phenomenal properties of experiences are *either* properties of experienced physical objects (in the case of nonhallucinatory experiences) *or* some other kind of thing (in the case of hallucinatory experiences). I adopt disjunctivism because it enables me to hold on to my direct realism, my view that the external objects we perceive are literally parts of our perceptual experiences of these objects, and therefore the observable properties of these objects can intelligibly determine the phenomenal properties of these experiences. And the reason I wish to hold on to my direct realism is to vindicate the familiar idea that the (external) world reveals itself to us in experience, an idea that requires that intelligible relations obtain between properties of external objects and properties of our experiences of those objects (sec. 1.5).[10]

I have defended disjunctivism elsewhere (1997) and will not repeat my arguments here. But let me say a little more about what I am committed to with respect to hallucinations and illusions. A hallucination is an experience in which no physical object appears to the subject, but it is not an experience in which no observable properties appear to the subject. Insofar as we are concerned with hallucinations that have the same kind of phenomenal properties as veridical experiences, the phenomenal properties of hallucinations will similarly be determined by (instantiated) observable properties. These observable properties are not instantiated in perceived physical objects, for when we hallucinate, we are not perceiving any physical objects. As a disjunctivist, I need not be committed to any particular positive account of how the observable properties associated with hallucinations are instantiated. I am mainly concerned in this book with nonhallucinatory experiences, and I will say little else about hallucinations.

I do want to say that the phenomenal properties of illusions *are* determined by observable properties of perceived physical objects. An illusion is naturally characterized as an experience in which a perceived physical object appears to have some observable property that it does not actually have. Such an illusion will presumably have a phenomenal property that corresponds to the observable property that the physical object appears to have but does not actually have. So how can I say that the phenomenal property in question is determined by an observable property of the perceived physical object? Consider the case of color illusions; consider, specifically, a white wall that looks red (under red light, say). In my view, the white wall is in fact instantiating the property of sensory redness; we have an illusion because the wall's redness does not correspond to what Colin McGinn calls the wall's "real color" (1983, 11). The wall's real color is white insofar as white is the sensory color the wall instantiates in normal conditions with respect to normal perceivers. The white wall looks red, and so the illusory experience instantiates the property of phenomenal redness. But the phenomenal redness *is* determined by the (sensory) redness of the wall, although the experience is illusory. What makes the experience illusory is not that the wall is not red but that its redness does not match the color it instantiates in normal conditions. More generally, despite what we may initially have thought, illusions are not experiences in which perceived physical objects lack the observable properties that are needed to determine the experiences' phenomenal properties. Rather, an illusion is an experience in which an observable property is perceived that does not match some related property of the perceived object.

Despite the differences between the view of the qualia theorist and my own view, we are both opposed to representationalism. We both share the view that phenomenal properties must be determined by instantiated (observable) properties, whereas the representationalist holds that phenomenal properties are determined by represented properties. I submit that reflection informs us that representationalism is mistaken. Reflection on the natures of observable properties and phenomenal properties reveals that observable properties (partly) determine phenomenal properties, and so it is reflection that informs us that representationalism, the view that phenomenal properties are solely determined by representational properties, is mistaken. I am not denying that experiences have representational properties: when I experience the redness of an object, I am typically aware of the object *as* being red, and to be aware of the object *as* being red is surely to represent it as being red. Nor do I deny that representational properties in part determine the nature of phenomenal properties; just as reflection on the natures of observable properties and phenomenal properties reveals an intelligible explanatory relation between them, so too reflection on the natures of representational properties and phenomenal properties also reveals an intelligible explanatory relation between them. Phenomenal properties are determined by both observable and representational properties; I am merely disputing the representationalist view that phenomenal properties are determined *solely* by representational properties. Compare experiences with conscious thoughts. Both are conscious mental states, and so both have what-it-is-like properties (i.e., phenomenal properties).[11] Moreover, both have representational properties: both an experience of red and a conscious thought of something red represent some object being red. But whereas the what-it-is-like properties of a thought are determined solely by the thought's representational properties, the what-it-is-like properties of an experience are not. What it is like for a subject to think that there is something red in the world is different from what it is like for a subject to experience something red in the world, and so the what-it-is-like properties of the thought and experience cannot be determined by the same kinds of properties. The experience of red and the conscious thought of something red both represent an object being red, but they differ in phenomenal character, even if we restrict ourselves to a consideration of the aspect of their phenomenal character that pertains to redness. The phenomenal character of the experience contains something that is lacking in the phenomenal character of the thought. When a subject experiences red, something *looks* or *appears* red to the subject, but nothing appears red to a subject when she is merely thinking with her eyes closed that something is red. This additional phenomenal property of the experience (what we have been calling phenomenal redness) cannot be determined by the experience's property of representing the color red, for the corresponding thought shares this representational property and yet lacks the phenomenal property. It must be something nonrepresentational that is determining the experience's phenomenal redness; I claim that it is an actual instantiation of redness in the world. Both experiences and thoughts represent things about the world, but only in experience does the world present itself to us. Only the what-it-is-like properties of experience are intelligibly related to observable properties of the world, and not merely to representational properties of the mind.[12]

I am arguing that representationalists cannot account for
the difference in phenomenal character between experiences
and (conscious) thoughts that share representational content.
Representationalists can acknowledge that there are differences
between experiences and thoughts other than their difference in
phenomenal character, and some have tried to appeal to such
differences to account for the differing phenomenal characters
of experiences and thoughts. Most obviously, an experience is
one kind of mental state, and a thought is a different kind of
mental state, and Michael Tye (1992, 166–167) has argued that
this difference in kind of mental state determines the difference
in phenomenal character between experiences and thoughts.
Similarly, Adam Pautz (2007, 519–520) claims that a subject having an experience stands in one kind of relation to the contents
of the experience, whereas a person having a thought stands in
a different kind of relation to the contents of the thought. It is
this difference in relation, according to Pautz, that determines
the difference in phenomenal character between experiences
and thoughts. Both of these representationalist proposals fail for
the same reason: they seek to employ a single difference between
experiences and thoughts to account for numerous phenomenal differences between experiences and thoughts. There is not
just one general difference between the phenomenal characters of experiences and thoughts; there are numerous particular differences. There is the phenomenal difference between an
experience of red and a thought of something red, there is the
phenomenal difference between an experience of blue and a
thought of something blue, and there is the phenomenal difference between an experience of a square object and a thought of
a square object. All are distinct differences. More generally there
is a distinct phenomenal difference for each observable property

that can be represented by experiences and thoughts. The qualia theorist employs a variety of qualia to account for these many differences; I employ the observable properties themselves. But the representationalist cannot account for these many phenomenal differences by means of a single difference between experiences and thoughts.[13]

What the representationalist needs are a variety of differences between experiences and thoughts to determine the many phenomenal differences between experiences and thoughts. And given that the representationalist holds that it is representational properties that determine phenomenal properties, these differences must be representational differences. In other words, the representationalist must hold that experiences and conscious thoughts represent different kinds of properties. Such a view seems extremely implausible, for it seems that "we can *think* that things are *exactly* as our experience represents them to be" (Jackson 2004, 434; italics in original).[14] The representationalist might appeal to nonconceptualism to try to make sense of this view. Nonconceptualism holds that experiences, but not thoughts, have nonconceptual representational content; thoughts, by contrast, merely have conceptual representational content. One way to understand this claim is to say that concepts literally enter into the representational content of thoughts, whereas things other than concepts enter into the representational content of experiences (Heck 2000). In other words, thoughts represent only concepts, whereas experiences (also) represent things other than concepts. These additional representational properties of experiences can then determine the phenomenal properties that experiences have but thoughts lack. Consider, again, an experience of red and a thought of something red. Presumably the nonconceptualist representationalist would say that the thought represents only the concept of red, not redness itself, whereas the experience does represent redness itself (i.e., the color red). This difference in representational properties is then supposed to explain the difference in phenomenal character between the experience and the thought. But surely we can think about colors as well as experience them; I can consciously think about my wife's red dress, even when I close my eyes. But if a thought of something red represents the color red as well as the concept of this color, then it is unclear what extra nonconceptual thing the experience of red represents that the thought does not. I conclude that nonconceptualism cannot be used to save representationalism.[15]

For the reasons thus set forth, I believe that representationalism fails; the phenomenal properties of experiences are not solely determined by their representational properties. Instead phenomenal properties (of experiences) are partly determined by, and, more generally, are intelligibly related to, their corresponding observable properties. Let us review what we know so far about these intelligible relations. Phenomenal properties are intelligibly similar in a certain way to their corresponding observable properties. But this similarity is of a special kind: in virtue of this similarity, observable properties are able to explain in an intelligible way the nature of their corresponding phenomenal properties. What it is like to experience red has the nature that it does because red has the nature that *it* does. So observable properties not only are intelligibly similar to corresponding phenomenal properties but also intelligibly explain those phenomenal properties.

What we want now is a better understanding of exactly how observable properties are similar to and explain their corresponding phenomenal properties; we want to articulate the nature of these intelligible relations. Further understanding is especially needed here because of the puzzling nature of these relations. How can observable properties be similar to phenomenal properties given that they are so different from each other? Generally when two or more properties are similar to each other, they are properties of the same kind, and the fact that they are properties of the same kind helps explain how they can be similar to each other. Red can be similar to orange because they are both colors; what it is like to experience red can be similar to what it is like to experience orange because they are both phenomenal colors. On the other hand, we don't expect there to be any interesting kind of similarity between red and the number 2 because they are such different kinds of things. And yet red is similar in an interesting and intelligible way to what it is like to experience red despite the fact that red is an observable property and what it is like to experience red is a phenomenal property, and observable properties and phenomenal properties are very different kinds of properties. We need to understand better the nature of the similarity between phenomenal properties and observable properties if we are not to be puzzled by the fact that there is a similarity here at all.

Phenomenal properties and observable properties are so different from each other because phenomenal properties are what-it-is-like properties and observable properties are not. Remember that, according to Nagel, "an organism has conscious mental states if and only if there is something it is like to *be* that organism—something it is like *for* the organism" (1974, 436). What Nagel is getting at here is how what-it-is-like properties differ from all other properties in the world, whether these other properties be reductive physical properties or sensory properties. In particular, whereas objects merely *have* these other properties, what-it-is-like properties exist *for* the subject that has them. The tomato just *is* red; the redness does not exist *for* the tomato, whereas there is something it is like *for* the subject to experience the redness of the tomato. The idea seems to be that what-it-is-like properties are so different from all other properties that the way they are instantiated in things differs from the way in which other properties are instantiated: they are instantiated *for* the subject that has them, not merely *in* the subject that has them. But given that what-it-is-like properties differ from other properties in such an extreme way, how can they be similar to any other kinds of properties in any kind of interesting way? We need to understand the nature of the similarity between phenomenal properties and observable properties if we are to be able to answer this question.

Similar questions arise when we focus on the explanatory relations between phenomenal properties and observable properties. Observable properties can intelligibly explain phenomenal properties in virtue of their similarity. But given that observable properties and phenomenal properties are also so different from each other, it is unclear *how* observable properties can explain the nature of their corresponding phenomenal properties. Given that red is not a what-it-is-like property, and phenomenal red is a what-it-is-like property, how can red intelligibly explain the nature of phenomenal red? Presumably observable properties only partly explain the nature of their corresponding phenomenal properties. But we will not understand even the nature of this partial explanation until we know what else is needed to explain phenomenal properties.

I have already noted that representational properties as well as observable properties determine phenomenal character. But representational properties are not the only additional elements needed to provide an intelligible explanation of phenomenal properties. Representational properties are not what-it-is-like properties, either; representational properties can be possessed by a variety of things other than conscious mental states (e.g., sentences, maps, paintings), and so they cannot be what-it-is-like properties. But then we still face the problem of how properties that are not what-it-is-like properties can intelligibly explain the nature of properties that are what-it-is-like properties. Let us now proceed to solve this problem.

2.3 How Observable Properties Intelligibly Explain Phenomenal Properties

Reflection reveals that the relation between observable property and corresponding phenomenal property is something like the (intelligible) relation between part and whole. (The same applies to the relation between representational property and corresponding phenomenal property.) We do not yet understand how an observable property intelligibly determines the nature of its corresponding phenomenal property because we do not yet have before us all the "parts" of this "whole." Redness is only one of the parts of phenomenal redness; if we are to understand how redness determines phenomenal redness, we also need to understand the part of phenomenal redness that contributes the "phenomenal" to phenomenal redness. In other words, red is not a what-it-is-like property, and phenomenal redness is; what we need to understand is how redness intelligibly combines with something else to produce a what-it-is-like property that is similar to redness. (The *combination* is intelligible insofar as it is an intelligible *fact* [sec. 1.1] that when redness combines with something else, it produces a what-it-is-like property that is similar to redness.)

But how does "what-it-is-likeness" get into the picture here? As noted earlier (sec. 2.1), a what-it-is-like property is the mark of a conscious mental state: a conscious state just is a state that has a what-it-is-like property. But the word "conscious" is not merely a label we use to refer to states that have what-it-is-like properties. Rather, consciousness is the element of conscious mental states that *explains* why such states have what-it-is-like properties; consciousness is the element of conscious mental states that contributes the "what-it-is-likeness" to the what-it-is-like properties of those states. So in the case of an experience of red, it is consciousness that combines with redness to give rise to phenomenal redness, the phenomenal property that is the intelligible result of this combination. (Again, the *result* is intelligible insofar as it is an intelligible fact that when consciousness combines with redness, the result is phenomenal redness.) Consciousness is the missing "part" of phenomenal properties, that part of phenomenal properties which enables us to understand how observable properties intelligibly determine the nature of phenomenal properties.

Just as reflection on the nature of a phenomenal property informs us of the nature of that observable property which intelligibly explains the nature of the phenomenal property, so too reflection on the nature of a phenomenal property informs us more inclusively that it is intelligibly explained by that observable property combined with consciousness. It is easy to miss the role of consciousness here, for consciousness plays the same explanatory role for every phenomenal property. Nevertheless consciousness plays an indispensable role here, for it is only the combination of an observable property with consciousness that results in a phenomenal property, a phenomenal property that is intelligibly similar to the observable property from which it is derived.

How exactly does consciousness figure in the nature of an experience? Observable properties are properties of the physical objects we experience, whereas phenomenal properties are properties of subjects of experience. So if observable properties are to help determine the phenomenal properties of experience, they need to be related to the subject of the experience. It is consciousness that relates the subject to these observable properties and to the physical objects that have them. Consciousness is a feature of experience that always occurs in relational form. Perceptual experience consists in a subject being conscious of observable properties being instantiated in a physical object, and the physical object is thereby part of the experience. The subject is engaged in an *act* of consciousness directed toward an *object* of consciousness.[16] Consciousness is a feature that enables a subject in effect to reach out toward the external world.

But there is more to an experience than a subject being conscious of an object; there is the phenomenal character of the experience. Recall that phenomenal properties are not structural properties (sec. 2.2). When a subject experiences the redness of an object, the subject does instantiate a structural property: the subject has the property of being related to the red object by means of an act of consciousness. But the subject also instantiates a phenomenal property that is distinct from this structural property, for in addition to the subject being an element in this structure (the structural property), there is also something it is like for the subject to be an element in this structure (the phenomenal property). The phenomenal property is distinct from the structural property, but it is intelligibly related to it, for it is the intelligible product of the elements of the structure. Phenomenal redness, that is, what it is like to be conscious of redness, is intelligibly explained by the combination of consciousness and redness in the structure of an experience of red. It is the nature of consciousness that an act of consciousness cannot obtain without there being a corresponding what-it-is-like property instantiated by the subject of that act of consciousness. The determinate nature of the what-it-is-like property of an experience will intelligibly depend on the nature of the observable properties to which the act of consciousness is directed. The observable properties can help determine the nature of the what-it-is-like property precisely because the subject is conscious of these observable properties. The nature of phenomenal redness, for example, will be intelligibly related to redness; phenomenal redness can be said to be the "what-it-is-like" version of redness. And generally, phenomenal properties can be thought of as determinate ways of being conscious.

Now that we understand how observable properties intelligibly explain phenomenal properties, we are also in a position to understand how the representational properties of an experience intelligibly contribute to its phenomenal character. Let us begin by specifying how representational properties figure in the structure of experience. Whereas the observable properties instantiated in an experience are properties of the object of consciousness, the representational properties of the experience are properties of the act of consciousness itself. It is part of the nature of experiential consciousness to be representational; experiential consciousness cannot but occur in a representational form. Experiential consciousness is always consciousness *as*; one cannot be conscious of an experienced object without being conscious of it *as* being a certain way, and to be conscious of it as being a certain way is to *represent* it as being that way. There are two kinds of representational content that an experience can have. First, the representational content of experience will always be partly demonstrative content. One is always conscious of the object of consciousness as being like *that*, where "that" refers to the instantiated observable properties toward which the act of consciousness is directed. In fact, it is because the representational content of experience is always partly demonstrative that observable properties can contribute to the phenomenal character of the experience: they can contribute because they are demonstrated. So when I experience the redness of an object and the object appears red to me, in the first instance the object appears red to me in virtue of the fact that I am conscious of the object as being like *that*, where "that" refers to the redness of the object of which I am conscious. But typically the representational content of an experience will include more than demonstrative content. Given that I am a knowledgeable individual who possesses concepts of observable properties, I will typically employ concepts of the appropriate observable properties to represent the object of consciousness. So when I experience the redness of an object, not only will I be conscious of the object as being like *that*; I will also be conscious of the object as being red, in the sense that I employ the concept of red to represent the object of my experience.[17] Thus an object can also appear red to me in virtue of the fact that I employ the concept of red to represent it in my experience.

Now, just as observable properties intelligibly determine aspects of phenomenal character, so too representational properties intelligibly determine aspects of phenomenal character. The observable properties of the object of consciousness intelligibly determine aspects of the subject's phenomenal character by being related to the subject through the subject's act of consciousness, and similarly representational properties intelligibly determine aspects of the subject's phenomenal character by being properties *of* the subject's act of consciousness. Consider an experience of red again. What it is like to have an experience of red is a matter of what it is like to be *conscious* of a *red object.* So the what-it-is-like property of this experience will be intelligibly determined both by representational properties of the act of consciousness and by observable properties of the red object of consciousness. In sum, we now understand how both observable properties and representational properties figure in the structure of experience, and therefore we can understand how both intelligibly contribute to the nature of phenomenal character.

I will continue to focus primarily on the contribution of observable properties rather than representational properties to phenomenal character, as my interest is in how experience intelligibly relates us to properties instantiated in the world. So let us summarize what we have learned in this section about how observable properties help to determine the nature of their corresponding phenomenal properties. We began with a problem: how can observable properties intelligibly explain the nature of corresponding phenomenal properties, given that observable properties and phenomenal properties are so different from each other? The solution is that an observable property gives rise to a corresponding phenomenal property by combining with an act of consciousness. When an act of consciousness is directed onto observable properties of some object of consciousness, a third thing results: a what-it-is-like property. There is something it is like for the subject to be conscious of those observable properties. This third thing is distinct both from the observable properties and from the act of consciousness directed onto those observable properties, but it is intelligibly related to them. Similarly, this third thing is something over and above the mere juxtaposition of the two items; rather, it is the intelligible result of the juxtaposition of the two items.

Recall the force of saying that phenomenal properties *intelligibly* result from the combination of observable properties with an act of consciousness. Intelligible relations can be discovered by reflection on the natures of their relata (they can be known a priori). So, for example, reflection on the natures of redness, phenomenal redness, and consciousness reveals that the nature of phenomenal redness is such as to result in an intelligible way from the combination of an act of consciousness directed at redness. The result is not only an intelligible one but a necessary one. Given the natures of redness and consciousness, it is necessary that their combination result in the instantiation of the phenomenal property we have been referring to as phenomenal redness. Earlier I stated that redness necessitates the nature of phenomenal redness (sec. 2.2); we now see that it would be more precise to say that the combination of redness with consciousness necessitates the nature of phenomenal redness. The nature of a phenomenal property is an intelligible function of the nature of consciousness and the nature of its corresponding observable property.

Do we now have a sufficient understanding of how observable properties intelligibly explain their corresponding phenomenal properties? Perhaps one might still want to know *how* the combination of consciousness with an observable property results in this new thing, a phenomenal property; what is the mechanism, so to speak? I believe that the request for a mechanism here is misplaced. Recall that when an act of consciousness combines with an observable property to produce a phenomenal property, it is something like parts combining to produce a whole. No mechanism is needed to explain how parts produce a whole; given that the parts exist in suitable relations to each other, the object comprising those parts automatically exists, as well. It is just the nature of a whole to be determined by the existence of its parts (in suitable relations to each other). Similarly, when a subject is conscious of observable properties, it is automatically the case that the subject has a corresponding what-it-is-like property: there is something it is like for the subject to be conscious of those observable properties. No mechanism is needed to explain how the subject comes to have a what-it-is-like property, for it is just the nature of an act of consciousness that it can obtain only if the subject of that act of consciousness has an appropriate what-it-is-like property, one whose nature is intelligibly determined (in the case of perceptual experience) by the observable properties to which the act of consciousness is directed.

I do not mean to minimize the differences between the two cases. Insofar as the relation between a whole and its parts is an intelligible relation, it is intelligible because the whole is nothing over and above the sum of its parts, whereas the phenomenal character of an experience is something over and above the subject of that experience engaged in an act of consciousness directed toward the object of that experience. So we must account for this additional thing in the case of the phenomenal character of an experience. But my point is that we don't need to search for some hidden causal mechanism to account for the production of this additional thing, for the *nature* of consciousness is such that the mere combination of an act of consciousness with observable properties is sufficient to result in the instantiation of this additional thing. There is nothing *mysterious* about the production of phenomenal character that suggests the existence of some hidden mechanism responsible for such production; on the contrary, it is *intelligible* that the combination of an act of consciousness with observable properties results in the instantiation of phenomenal properties that are intelligibly related to those observable properties. It is just the nature of consciousness to attach itself to observable properties and produce from them their phenomenal counterparts. Or, as I suggest in the following section, it is the nature of consciousness to attach itself to the world and reveal its nature to us.

Toward the end of section 2.2, I noted that we needed a better understanding of the intelligible relations that hold between observable properties and their corresponding phenomenal properties. In this section, I attempted to articulate the nature of the intelligible *explanatory* relations that hold between observable properties and phenomenal properties. In the following section, I begin to explore further the nature of the intelligible *similarity* relations that hold between observable and phenomenal properties.

2.4 How Observable Properties Are Intelligibly Similar to Phenomenal Properties

It is the nature of consciousness to attach itself to observable properties and produce from them corresponding phenomenal properties. But what is the nature of the correspondence here; how is phenomenal redness, say, similar to redness? We already know *that* observable properties are similar to phenomenal properties, but we have not yet specified the way in which they are similar. Moreover, we have already noted a difficulty we face in attempting to specify the way in which they are similar: how can observable and phenomenal properties be similar in any interesting way given how different they are from each other? Specifically, phenomenal properties are what-it-is-like properties; observable properties are not; and given the distinctive nature of what-it-is-like properties, it is unclear how they can be similar in any interesting way to properties that are not what-it-is-like properties.

I think that we can begin to address this problem if we focus on what makes what-it-is-like properties so distinctive. The idea mentioned earlier is that what-it-is-like properties are so different from other properties that they need to be instantiated differently from the way other properties are instantiated: other properties are instantiated *in* objects, whereas what-it-is-like properties are instantiated *for* subjects (sec. 2.2). Now consider an observable property, redness, and its corresponding what-it-is-like property, phenomenal redness (what it is like to be conscious of redness). I suggest that the *only* difference between these two properties is in the ways they are instantiated: redness is instantiated *in* objects; phenomenal redness is instantiated *for* subjects. In other words, there are not really two distinct properties here; there is a single property instantiated in two different ways. When the property is instantiated in the standard way *in* an object, we talk of a red object; when the property is instantiated *for* a subject, we talk of there being something it is like for that subject to be conscious of a red object. The difference between redness and phenomenal redness is not the difference between two properties but the difference between two different kinds of instantiation of the same property. An instance of redness is similar to an instance of phenomenal redness in that they are instances of the same property, but instantiated in different ways. More generally, my suggestion is that a phenomenal property is similar to its corresponding observable property in that they are literally the same property, but instantiated in different ways.

Although I am claiming that the difference between a phenomenal property and its corresponding observable property is not in fact a difference in properties but a difference in kinds of instantiation of the same property, nevertheless, in contexts where no misunderstandings will arise, I will continue to employ standard terminology and speak of phenomenal and observable *properties*, as opposed to, say, phenomenal and observable *instantiations*. At other times, I make clear that what we have here are different instantiations of the same property. Note that it does not matter how we refer to this property. Once we say that some phenomenal property is identical to its corresponding observable property, we are free to refer to this single property in any way we want, so long as we are clear about what we are doing. We can refer to this property as an observable property, or a phenomenal property, or we can invent some new terminology to refer to it. Nevertheless I typically refer to it as an observable property and say that a phenomenal property just is an observable property that is instantiated in a special kind of way. For example, I will say that phenomenal redness just is redness that is instantiated in a certain kind of way; I will not say that redness just is phenomenal redness instantiated in a certain kind of way. I think that the first formulation is more perspicuous than the second in that it highlights the asymmetric nature of the intelligible relations between phenomenal properties and their corresponding observable properties (sec. 2.2). Recall that observable properties determine phenomenal properties, not vice versa. Observable properties intelligibly combine with consciousness to give rise to phenomenal properties (sec. 2.3), phenomenal properties that can be characterized as observable properties that are instantiated in a special, "conscious" way.

One might think that the idea that properties can be instantiated in two distinct ways is a radical modification of our commonsense metaphysics that we should adopt only with the utmost caution. But perhaps we need to be a little creative here. We need to make sense of the initially puzzling idea that consciousness brings something essentially new into the world (phenomenal character, subjectivity), but at the same time this something new is intelligibly related to the observable properties already present in the world. I am suggesting that if we think of phenomenal properties as observable properties instantiated in a new, distinctive way, then we will be able to make sense of this puzzling idea.

Moreover, I deny that the notion of a second kind of instantiation relation revises our commonsense metaphysics. I believe that we are already implicitly committed to this idea. As noted earlier, we commonly say that in experience the world reveals itself to us and makes itself manifest to us (sec. 1.5). But what does it really mean to say the world reveals itself to us in experience? It is only certain parts of the world that reveal themselves to us in experience, certain observable parts. In particular, certain observable properties of these parts reveal themselves to us. And what does it mean to say these observable properties reveal themselves to us? I submit that when we say the world reveals itself to us in experience, we are just saying that these observable properties are instantiated in experience in a special kind of way, a way that deserves to be characterized in terms of the idea of revealing. This special kind of instantiation counts as "revealing" because its nature is such as to inform us of the presence of the properties that are instantiated in this way. When I am conscious of the redness of an object, and there is something it is like for me to be conscious of the redness of the object, the redness enters into a special relation with me. Although the redness is a property of some object external to me and is instantiated in the standard way in that external object, the redness also exists *for me*, and therefore I can know that the external object is red, and I can know what it is for an external object to be red. The redness of the object is *revealed* to me, in that there is an intelligible connection between the way the redness of the object exists for me (it exists for me in the form of phenomenal redness) and my ability to obtain knowledge of the object's redness.

The difficulty at the beginning of this section was to understand the way in which phenomenal properties are similar to observable properties. I suggested that phenomenal properties are similar to observable properties in that they just are observable properties, but instantiated in a distinct kind of way. The usefulness of the suggestion is that it will enable us to understand how experience enables us to obtain knowledge of objects' observable properties. I develop this connection between experience and knowledge in the next two chapters.

2.5   How Consciousness Reveals the External World to Us: A First Step

So far we have focused on phenomenal properties that are intelligibly related to observable properties. We have also briefly discussed phenomenal properties that are intelligibly related to representational properties. But there is more to the phenomenal character of a perceptual experience than these two kinds of phenomenal properties. Not only does experience reveal to us the presence of observable properties; it also reveals the observable properties to be properties of *external*, that is, independently existing, objects. The external world itself reveals itself to us in experience, not merely its observable properties: we experience what appear to be independently existing objects. When we experience observable properties, the properties *appear* to be instantiated in objects, and the objects *look like* independently existing objects. So just as there are phenomenal properties that are intelligibly related to observable properties, so too there is an aspect of phenomenal character—let's call it *phenomenal externality*—that is intelligibly related to the property of externality, the property of being an independently existing object.

What exactly is the property of phenomenal externality? Just as phenomenal redness is the property of what it is like to experience redness, so too phenomenal externality is the property of what it is like to experience an external object. And what *is* it like to experience an external object? One cannot experience an external object without experiencing observable properties of that object. So we can say that what it is like to experience an external object is a matter of its experienced observable properties *appearing* to be properties of an external object. But what is the nature of this kind of appearance? Consider an experience of a red external object. The subject's act of consciousness will be directed at multiple instantiations of the property of redness located in a continuous two-dimensional region of space that is itself located in our familiar three-dimensional space.[18] Now, one aspect of the phenomenal character of this experience is phenomenal redness. Phenomenal redness just is the property of redness instantiated in that special way characteristic of phenomenal properties; it is the property of redness existing *for* the subject of the experience (sec. 2.4). So we can say that the phenomenal character of the experience at least includes multiple instantiations of the property of redness existing at a two-dimensional region of space and existing *for* the subject of the experience. But this is not a complete description of the phenomenal character of the experience, for it does not capture the *unity* of the phenomenal character. There is more to the phenomenal character of the experience than a multitude of instantiations of redness at various points in space existing for a subject: this multitude of instantiations exists for the subject as one, unified entity. And what is the nature of this unity? I submit that the unity in question is constituted by the instantiation of the property of phenomenal externality: the instantiations of redness *appear* to the subject to be instantiated in a single external object.

Let me elaborate on the way in which the unity of the phenomenal character is constituted by the instantiation of the property of phenomenal externality. The redness of which the subject is conscious looks to be the redness of an external object in that it looks to be the redness of the facing surface of an external object. The instantiations of redness do not appear as a multitude of distinct colored points or regions; they appear as one, colored, two-dimensional surface. But furthermore, they appear as a two-dimensional surface that is part of one three-dimensional object, an object that also has parts that do not appear. The instantiations of redness appear as one part of a single object with many parts, parts that unite to form a single object. Thus they appear as part of an object that depends for its existence on its parts being related to each other in an appropriate way. But insofar as the object is *constituted* by its parts, its existence depends *only* on its parts being related to each other in the appropriate way; its existence will not depend on anything else, including the subject of the experience. So the redness looks to the subject to be the redness of an object that exists independently of the subject; in other words, the redness looks to be the redness of an external object.

Now that we understand what phenomenal externality is, we can turn to its explanation. Observable properties combined with consciousness intelligibly give rise to corresponding phenomenal properties; can we give a similar account to explain phenomenal externality? Yes; just as phenomenal redness, say, is intelligibly explained by redness, so too can phenomenal externality be intelligibly explained by externality (the property of being an external object). In other words, the fact that some experienced observable properties *appear* to be properties of some external object can be intelligibly explained by the fact that they *are* properties of an external object. Phenomenal externality constitutes the unity of phenomenal character, and such unity can intelligibly be explained by a corresponding unity of observable properties, such unity consisting in the observable properties being unified in an actually existing external object. A nonhallucinatory experience consists in a subject being conscious of observable properties instantiated in an external physical object, and it is the presence of that external object that intelligibly explains why the observable properties appear to be properties of an external object. But although phenomenal externality *can* be intelligibly explained by externality, externality cannot be the only explanation of phenomenal externality. Externality is not a feature of hallucinatory experiences, although phenomenal externality sometimes is a feature of such experiences. When I hallucinate, no external object is present to me (the property of externality is not instantiated), even though it may *appear* to me as if an external object is present to me (the property of phenomenal externality is instantiated). I leave open the question of what explains the phenomenal externality of such hallucinatory experiences; we need not resolve this question for the purposes of this book.[19]

I began this section by claiming that phenomenal externality is intelligibly related to the property of externality. It is worth noting how the way in which the property of phenomenal externality is intelligibly related to the property of externality is somewhat different from the way in which the phenomenal properties with which we are already familiar are intelligibly related to their corresponding observable properties. Specifically, whereas these latter phenomenal properties must always be explained by their corresponding observable properties (sec. 2.2), phenomenal externality, as we have just seen, is not always to be explained in terms of the property of externality. Nevertheless phenomenal externality *can* be intelligibly explained by externality, because phenomenal externality is intelligibly similar to externality. How is phenomenal externality similar to externality? In the previous section, I suggested that phenomenal properties are similar to their corresponding nonphenomenal properties in that they just are these nonphenomenal properties instantiated in a special way characteristic of phenomenal properties. So just as phenomenal redness, say, is the property of redness instantiated in this special way, so too phenomenal externality just is the property of externality instantiated in the special way characteristic of phenomenal properties.

I also suggested in the previous section that phenomenal properties *reveal* the presence of their corresponding nonphenomenal properties, in that their nature is such as to enable us to obtain knowledge of the presence of their corresponding nonphenomenal properties. Now suppose that one is willing to endorse this suggestion for phenomenal properties other than the property of phenomenal externality. Nevertheless, given the difference I just noted between phenomenal externality and other phenomenal properties, one might not be willing to endorse this suggestion for the property of phenomenal externality. Whereas other phenomenal properties cannot be

instantiated in the absence of their corresponding nonphenomenal properties being instantiated, the property of phenomenal
externality can be instantiated in the absence of the property
of externality being instantiated (i.e., in hallucinatory experiences). So even in those nonhallucinatory cases in which both
the property of phenomenal externality and the property of
externality are instantiated, it might be unclear how the nature
of phenomenal externality can be such as to enable us to *know*
that the property of externality is instantiated. That is, it might
be unclear how the nature of our experiences can be such as to
enable us to know that there is an external world at all. I respond
to this skeptical concern at various points in the course of the
next two chapters. More generally, I argue that despite the difference just noted between phenomenal externality and other
phenomenal properties, *all* phenomenal properties are such as
to enable us to obtain knowledge of the presence of their corresponding nonphenomenal properties.

3 The Intelligibility of Consciousness II: The Causal Powers of Conscious States

3.1 The Idea of Intelligible Causation

In this chapter, I explore and defend the idea that intelligible relations obtain between some of the causal properties of conscious states and the intrinsic noncausal properties that ground them. Like the intelligible relations between observable properties and phenomenal properties discussed in the previous chapter, these intelligible relations are supposed to be explanatory relations: the intrinsic properties in question are not themselves causal powers but are supposed to intelligibly explain why the relevant conscious states have some of their causal powers. The causal powers can be said to flow in an intelligible way from the intrinsic properties that ground them. I will say that when a causal power is intelligibly explained by the intrinsic property that grounds it, the causal power in question is an *intelligible* causal power. And the causation that results when an intelligible causal power is exercised is *intelligible causation*.

Let us distinguish between brute causation and intelligible causation. Entities have causal powers in virtue of certain of their categorical (i.e., noncausal) intrinsic properties; these categorical properties can be said to ground or underlie the relevant causal powers. But how are these categorical properties supposed to explain the causal powers that they ground? The philosophical consensus is that nothing about the intrinsic nature of these categorical properties explains how they ground causal powers; rather, causal powers are connected to their underlying categorical properties by means of something extrinsic: laws of nature. These laws of nature ensure that entities with such and such categorical properties will also have such and such causal powers. So causal powers will be explained by their underlying categorical properties together with laws of nature. For our purposes, we need not worry about what exactly laws of nature are supposed to be. What is relevant for our purposes is that according to this consensus view, laws of nature are *brute*, that is, *not intelligible*: they cannot be known a priori.[1] Mere reflection on a categorical property will not inform us of the causal powers (if any) that it grounds, for there is nothing about the nature of a categorical property that intelligibly explains how it grounds causal powers. Similarly, reflection on a causal power will not inform us of the nature of the categorical properties that ground it. Rather, to discover laws of nature, we need empirical knowledge about which categorical properties are constantly conjoined with which causal powers. A causal power that is explained in terms of underlying categorical properties together with brute laws of nature is a brute causal power, and the exercise of such a causal power is brute causation. The reigning philosophical consensus is that all causation is brute causation.

I respectfully disagree. I acknowledge that all (reductive) physical causation is brute causation. Natural science is the discipline that discovers physical causes, and natural science is an empirical discipline. But I wish to suggest that some mental causation is not brute but intelligible. What is characteristic of brute causation is that the explanatory connection between causal power and underlying categorical property is not intelligible but instead mediated by a brute law of nature, whereas I claim that some causal powers of conscious states are intelligible, in that an intelligible explanatory connection exists between them and their underlying categorical properties.[2] The connection is intelligible in that it can be known a priori (sec. 1.1); it can be known a priori that certain categorical mental properties ground certain causal powers. Something about the intrinsic nature of these categorical mental properties intelligibly explains how and why they ground certain kinds of causal powers. So mere reflection on these mental properties can inform us of the causal powers that they intelligibly support.

Insofar as we begin to understand the intelligible causal powers of conscious states, we also begin to understand why consciousness is so important to us (sec. 1.1). In the previous chapter, we examined how the phenomenal properties of our experiences are intelligibly related to the observable properties of the external world; we examined how phenomenal properties are the intelligible result of the combination of these properties with acts of consciousness. The wonder evoked in us when we consider these intelligible relations is a kind of aesthetic wonder. Dualists have traditionally emphasized how consciousness differs from everything else in the world, and rightly so. But what makes consciousness so wonderful is that despite being so different from everything else in the (external) world, it nevertheless intelligibly relates us to the external world, by combining with the external world to produce phenomenal properties. We marvel at this aesthetic feat of consciousness, the way it intelligibly combines such disparate kinds of entities. But our appreciation of the intelligibility of consciousness is not limited to this detached aesthetic wonder. Insofar as consciousness has intelligible causal powers, we are implicated more directly and actively in the intelligibility of consciousness. The intelligible causal powers of conscious states are, of course, *our* intelligible causal powers. Our actions are often caused by the exercise of these intelligible causal powers,[3] and we can thereby be said to act in intelligible ways, in ways that *make sense*, so to speak. And insofar as our lives are the sum of our actions, our very lives will make a kind of sense. Our lives do not consist in mere arbitrary sequences of events; on the contrary, many of the events of our lives are intelligible results of previous events. We act in intelligible ways, and our lives are thereby suffused with intelligibility.

In celebrating the fact that we have intelligible causal powers, I do not mean at all to minimize the importance of the intelligible relations described in chapter 2. By describing in the previous chapter the intelligible relations between the phenomenal properties of experiences and the observable properties of the external world, I succeeded in characterizing the intrinsic nature of phenomenal properties (sec. 2.4). In this chapter, I proceed to describe how this intrinsic nature intelligibly grounds some of the causal powers of experiences. The two kinds of intelligibility are intimately related. It is because the phenomenal properties of experiences are intelligibly related to properties of the world that experiences can intelligibly produce beliefs that constitute knowledge of these properties of the world.

My main task in this chapter is to articulate the nature of the intelligible relations that hold between some of the causal powers of our mental states and the intrinsic categorical properties that ground these powers. Many philosophers would strongly resist the idea that there can even be such a thing as intelligible causation; as noted earlier, the philosophical consensus is that all causation is brute causation. So before proceeding to my main task, let me make a few remarks to counter this resistance to the idea of intelligible causation.

3.2   Motivating the Idea of Intelligible Causation

Ultimately I cannot prove by argument that intelligible relations obtain between some of the causal powers of our mental states and the categorical properties that ground them. I can only ask that you reflect on the causal powers that I discuss and their underlying categorical properties, and hope that you detect the intelligible relations that hold between them. I cannot guarantee success; intelligible relations *can* be detected by reason, but not every attempt to detect them succeeds. But I can try to make those who resist the idea of intelligible causal powers more receptive to it, so that they will be more likely to find such powers when they look for them. In other words, I can attempt to lower resistance to the idea of intelligible causation.

What is the source of the resistance to the idea of intelligible causation? Perhaps some of this resistance reflects a more general resistance to the idea that necessary connections can obtain between distinct existences (sec. 1.2). A causal power and its underlying categorical property are two distinct properties (existences). Moreover, insofar as an intelligible connection obtains between these two distinct properties, the connection will also be a necessary one. Insofar as the connection is intelligible, something about the intrinsic nature of the underlying categorical property will intelligibly explain why it grounds the relevant causal power. And since the intrinsic nature of the categorical property is part of its essential nature, the intelligible connection between the categorical property and the causal power will also

be a necessary connection. So those who reject necessary connections between distinct existences will also reject intelligible
causation.

I have already pointed out that we have no reason to reject
necessary connections between distinct existences (sec. 1.2).
Moreover, we should not be suspicious of such necessary connections because of their unfamiliarity, for we saw in chapter 2
that such necessary connections are not unfamiliar. Specifically,
familiar *similarity* relations between properties are necessary relations between distinct existences, in those cases when the properties in question are distinct. The similarity relations between
red and orange (and between phenomenal redness and phenomenal orange) are examples of such relations. So we should have
no difficulty with the idea that there can be necessary connections between distinct existences.

Many philosophers specifically reject the idea of intelligible
causation regardless of whether they in general reject necessary
connections between distinct existences. Insofar as some categorical property intelligibly grounds some causal power, we
can know that it does so by a priori reflection on that categorical property. But many philosophers take David Hume to have
shown that we cannot have a priori knowledge of causal powers,
and therefore they reject the idea that there can be intelligible
causation. They accept the Humean view that all causation is
brute causation.

Hume's view does not merit its popularity. Although Hume
claims that we cannot have a priori knowledge of the causal
powers of anything,[4] he has by no means adequately supported
this claim. Hume is trying to "prove a negative"; his strategy
for doing so is to consider a wide variety of categorical properties, to insist that we can obtain no a priori knowledge of causal

powers that flow from those categorical properties, and then to argue that the representative nature of those categorical properties provides good inductive evidence for the general claim that we can have no a priori knowledge of the causal powers of anything.[5] But in fact the categorical properties that Hume considers are not sufficiently representative, for the only mental categorical properties that he considers are the categorical properties of acts of volition.[6] I, on the other hand, argue that the categorical properties of experiences (sec. 3.3), conscious beliefs (3.4), rational intuitions (3.5), conscious desires (5.2), pains and pleasures (5.3), and feelings (5.4) all intelligibly ground causal powers. Surely it does not follow from the fact that the categorical properties of acts of volition do not intelligibly ground causal powers that no categorical properties of conscious mental states intelligibly ground causal powers. In sum, Hume has not shown that all causation is brute causation.

Now, even if we accept that Hume has not proven that there is no such thing as intelligible causation, I suspect that many will still be reluctant to accept its existence. Perhaps it is the seeming unfamiliarity of the idea that makes some philosophers uncomfortable. For here I am claiming that reason, something we all possess, can detect intelligible connections between familiar mental categorical properties and familiar mental causal properties. But if we are all capable of detecting such connections, why have we not yet done so? I claim that we have done so; we are just not explicitly aware of having done so. Recall that I am not claiming to have discovered the intelligible features of consciousness; I am only attempting to articulate the nature of intelligible features of which we all have some kind of partial, implicit understanding (sec. 1.5). And I believe that we all do have such understanding of the intelligible causal powers of conscious states.

How is such implicit understanding expressed? We do not explicitly describe causal powers as intelligible, but we describe our conscious lives in ways that seem to imply the presence of intelligible causal powers. For example, as noted earlier, we say that the world reveals itself to us in experience (sec. 1.5, 2.4). Let us examine this statement somewhat more carefully than we have yet done. The statement is puzzling, for it is not literally true. Revealing is an intentional action; the physical objects we experience are not really capable of revealing anything to anyone. It is persons who reveal things: a person takes off his clothes and reveals his body, or he says something and reveals what he is thinking or some secret about himself. Insofar as we say that the world reveals itself to us in experience, it is because reason detects something about the nature of experience that is similar to what occurs in genuine cases of revealing. We detect a similarity here but have difficulty getting an explicit understanding of its nature; it is here that the philosopher comes in to help us understand and articulate the nature of this similarity. It is the nature of (genuine) revealing that it can give rise to knowledge. If I reveal something to you, then you are in a position to obtain knowledge of what I reveal. Moreover, the connection between revealing and knowledge is an intelligible one: it makes sense that I can know something if you have revealed it to me. Nevertheless the intelligibility here is of a trivial kind, for it stems from a definition. It is part of the meaning of "revealing" that a revealing is an action that can give rise to knowledge; we will not describe an action as a revealing of something unless we already believe that the action is one that can produce knowledge. So how are experiences similar to genuine cases of revealing? I submit that one aspect of the similarity that reason detects between experiences and genuine cases of revealing is that both can produce knowledge. Moreover, just as an intelligible connection holds between revealing and knowledge, so too an intelligible connection holds between experience and knowledge: that experiences have the power to produce knowledge is intelligible. But whereas the intelligible connection between revealing and knowledge is trivial, in that it stems from a definition, the intelligible connection between experience and knowledge is substantive, in that it stems from a necessary connection between two distinct existences in the world. Reason detects something about the intrinsic nature of experience that intelligibly explains how it is able to produce knowledge. A substantive intelligible connection holds here between two distinct properties of experience: some intrinsic categorical property of experience, and its causal power to produce knowledge. So in saying that the world is revealed to us in experience, we express the insight of reason that experiences can intelligibly produce knowledge. The idea that conscious states have intelligible causal powers does not originate with myself;[7] rather, it is implicit in a familiar way we have of speaking about experience.

Now, although I am not claiming to be the first to have come up with the idea that conscious states have intelligible causal powers, I claim to be one of the few philosophers to take this idea implicit in our everyday thinking about experience and render it explicit. And some may think that this latter claim is just as problematic as the former, for if the idea that conscious states have intelligible causal powers has long been implicit in our everyday thinking, then surely by now it should have been a familiar subject of philosophical discussion. It is not; philosophers have not really explored the idea that conscious states have intelligible causal powers. But we should not be surprised that philosophers have not explored this idea, given the philosophical consensus that all causation is brute causation. (I have already argued that this consensus is not supported by argument.) Let us not infer that anything is wrong with the idea that conscious states have intelligible causal powers from the fact that philosophers have not spent much time discussing it. That philosophers have resisted this idea in the past is no reason to continue to resist it in the present.

Moreover, although philosophers have not explicitly addressed this idea, much in the philosophical literature hints at it. Think of the traditional philosophical view that a subject who experiences an object is thereby *acquainted* with the object, or, equivalently, the object is thereby *given* to the subject.[8] These traditional ideas of acquaintance and the given are supposed to explain how experiences of an object give rise to thoughts and knowledge of that object. Because a subject is acquainted with an object, he is supposed to be able to think about it and know its nature. Now, what such talk of acquaintance and the given really amounted to was notoriously obscure, and so it was also obscure how the ideas of acquaintance and the given were supposed to explain thought and knowledge. These ideas were extensively criticized and today are in disrepute.[9] But I submit that these ideas were never really given their due. I have argued that an experience involves a subject engaged in an act of consciousness directed toward an object of consciousness; in brief, an experiencing subject is conscious of an object (sec. 2.3). Admittedly, to say that the experiencing subject is acquainted with an object does not seem to add anything to the description of the subject as being conscious of the object; the idea of acquaintance does not seem to point to any features of the experience that have not already been described. But it seems to me that advocates of the ideas of acquaintance and the given were not attempting to point to some as yet undiscovered intrinsic feature of experience; rather, they were attempting to point to the feature of experience, whatever it might be, that could (intelligibly) explain why experiences are able to produce thoughts and knowledge. They were groping toward the idea that the causal powers of experience to produce thoughts and knowledge about the experienced object are intelligible causal powers, powers that flow in an intelligible way from underlying categorical properties of experience. They were not able to pinpoint the relevant categorical properties or to articulate the nature of the intelligible connection between those categorical properties and the causal powers at issue. But they did seem to grasp that there is something special about these causal powers, something special about how they relate to their underlying categorical properties. In effect, to say that an experiencing subject is acquainted with an experienced object is just to say that something about the subject's relation to that object intelligibly explains why the subject can think and obtain knowledge about the object. The ideas of acquaintance and the given are naturally taken as tentative initial attempts to formulate the view that experiences have intelligible causal powers.

There are other indications that the view that conscious states have intelligible causal powers lies just beneath the surface of our philosophical thinking about the mind. As David Chalmers has noted, many philosophers find epiphenomenalism, the view that mental states do not have causal powers, to be "counterintuitive and repugnant" (1996, 150). But why should so many of us find this view to be repugnant? Note that the claim is not merely that we believe that epiphenomenalism is false, or that we have an intuition that it is false; rather, the suggestion is that we find the view to be *repugnant*. Why should we have such an extreme negative reaction toward epiphenomenalism; why should we feel so strongly that epiphenomenalism is mistaken? I suggest that our negative attitude toward epiphenomenalism reflects our implicit belief that mental states have intelligible causal powers, for if we believed merely that mental states have brute causal powers, we would not regard epiphenomenalism with such repugnance. The belief that mental states have brute causal powers must be justified by empirical evidence. Given the ways that such evidence is defeasible, we should be happy to allow for the possibility that our belief is mistaken. But we do not happily allow for this possibility, for we reject epiphenomenalism as repugnant.

Epiphenomenalists typically attempt to explain away our intuitions against epiphenomenalism by suggesting that we mistakenly infer from the constant conjunction of certain kinds of mental states and other states (mental or physical) that the mental states are the causes of the other states. The inference is mistaken, according to the epiphenomenalist, because in fact the two constantly conjoined states are both effects of a common physical cause.[10] Such an account of our anti-epiphenomenalist intuitions is unpersuasive: if our only evidence against epiphenomenalism were observations of constant conjunction, then epiphenomenalism would not seem so repugnant to us, for there are all sorts of cases where we are happy to acknowledge that a's and b's are constantly conjoined without a causal relation existing between them. Rather, our belief that mental states have causal powers is justified by a priori reflection on the categorical properties of our conscious mental states. Such reflection informs us that some of these categorical properties intelligibly ground causal powers; it thereby informs us that certain of our conscious mental states have intelligible causal powers.

Epiphenomenalism strikes us as counterintuitive because it runs *counter* to our rational *intuitions*, intuitions that are the product of our a priori reflection. It strikes us as repugnant because it renders the world less intelligible; it denies intelligibility where our reason has found it. In short, we feel so strongly that mental states have causal powers because reflection has shown us that the intrinsic nature of some of our mental states is such that they intelligibly ground causal powers; the causal powers flow in an intelligible way from their intrinsic nature.[11]

As I have said, for the most part we have not succeeded in explicitly articulating the idea that mental states have intelligible causal powers. Nevertheless I claim that it is our implicit commitment to this idea that accounts for our repugnance toward epiphenomenalism. I would also suggest that our implicit commitment to this idea explains some of the attraction of (analytic) functionalism. According to functionalism, our concept of an experience or some other kind of mental state is "a concept of a state that occupies a certain causal role, a state with certain typical causes and effects" (Lewis 1980, 218). So according to functionalism, not only will it be true that mental states have causal powers, but it will be a necessary (analytic) truth that mental states have causal powers. It is certainly not at all obvious that functionalism accurately captures the way we understand our mental terminology,[12] so why have so many been attracted to functionalism? Perhaps they sense that something is right about the functionalist's claim that it is necessary that certain mental states have certain causal powers. And I agree that there is something right about this claim; the claim is correct, but not for the reasons put forward by the functionalist. It is correct because mental states have intelligible causal powers; as we saw earlier in this section, if the causal powers of a mental state flow in an intelligible way from the intrinsic (and essential) nature of that mental state, then it will be necessary that the mental state has those causal powers. The functionalist mistakenly thinks that it is a necessary *analytic* truth that certain mental states have certain causal powers, whereas I am arguing that it is a necessary *synthetic* truth: there is a substantive necessary connection between the causal powers of some mental states and their underlying categorical properties. Nevertheless the functionalist should be credited with the insight that there is a necessary truth here, for up until now it has only been the functionalist who has defended the necessity of this truth.

Despite its problems, functionalism attracts many of us because of its claim that certain mental states necessarily have certain causal powers; many of us are attracted to this claim because of our implicit commitment to the idea that mental states have intelligible causal powers. We *should* express this commitment by embracing the view that it is a necessary *synthetic* truth that certain mental states have certain causal powers, but given the prevailing philosophical consensus against a priori synthetic knowledge, some of us mistakenly express this commitment by affirming the functionalist view that the aforementioned truth is a necessary *analytic* truth. But there is no more reason to reject a priori synthetic knowledge than there is to reject necessary connections between distinct existences.[13] Once we acknowledge that necessary (synthetic) connections can hold between distinct existences (sec. 1.2), we have no reason not to acknowledge that reason can discover such connections (assuming that they are intelligible). And when reason does discover such connections, it will have obtained a priori synthetic knowledge. Functionalism is not at all plausible as a thesis about meaning, so the best explanation of its attraction is to see it as a misguided attempt to do justice to our intuition that mental states necessarily have some of their causal powers. Of course, the more appropriate way to do justice to this intuition is explicitly to own up to the insight that underlies it: mental states have *intelligible* causal powers.

We need finally to overcome our resistance to the idea of intelligible causation. We have no good philosophical reasons to reject it. We need not fear it as something unfamiliar, for it is not unfamiliar. On the contrary, it is reflected in familiar, everyday ways of speaking about experience, and it lurks just beneath the surface of our philosophical discourse about mental states. Let us bring this idea to the surface and examine it more closely.

3.3   The Intelligible Causal Powers of Experiences

We have already seen how the idea that experiences have intelligible causal powers is implicit in the ways we speak about experience. Specifically, when we say that the world reveals itself to us in experience, we imply that experiences have the intelligible causal power to produce knowledge. Since our knowledge is constituted by a subset of our beliefs, to say that experiences have the intelligible power to produce knowledge is at least to say that experiences have the intelligible power to produce certain kinds of beliefs. What kinds of beliefs? Beliefs that reflect those aspects of the world revealed to us in experience. What is revealed to us in a (nonhallucinatory) experience is the object of the experience and observable properties of that object. So an experience has the intelligible power to produce perceptual beliefs to the effect that the object of experience has the observable properties in question. Such beliefs will express singular propositions of the form Fa, where a refers to the object of experience, and F

designates some observable property instantiated in the experience by the object of the experience. For example, I experience the redness of an object, and I immediately believe: *that* object is red. Of course, almost all philosophers would acknowledge that experiences have the causal power to produce such beliefs. I am attempting to make plausible the idea that the causal power in question is an *intelligible* causal power. An intelligible connection exists between the intrinsic nature of an experience and its causal power to produce these kinds of beliefs. My aim in this section is to articulate the nature of this intelligible connection. What is it about this connection that makes it intelligible? How does the causal power flow in an intelligible way from the intrinsic nature of the experience?

The causal power in question can be thought of as combining two distinct causal powers. A subject who believes a proposition of the form *Fa* both refers to the object *a* and attributes the property *F* to that object. So we can say that a subject's experience has both the power to produce in the subject an ability to refer to the object of experience, and the power to cause the subject to attribute some appropriate observable property to that object. I will examine each of these causal powers in turn.

3.3.1   The Experience's Power to Produce an Ability to Refer to the Object of Experience

What is it about an experience that intelligibly explains how it causes the subject of the experience to acquire an ability to refer to the object of the experience? The experiencing subject is conscious of the experienced object (sec. 2.3), and the traditional view seems to be that the subject is able to refer in thought to that object because he is conscious of it. Suppose, for example, that I am having a perceptual experience of a tomato; according to my direct realist view (sec. 2.2, 2.3), I am conscious of the tomato, and so I can refer to the tomato by, say, thinking, "That tomato is a striking shade of red." But why does consciousness of an object enable us to refer to it? According to H. H. Price, when the subject is conscious of an object in experience, the object is "brought before the [subject's] mind," and therefore the subject is able to think about it.[14] The difficulty here is in making sense of this talk of an object being before a subject's mind. Price apparently holds that something about the nature of the reference relation requires a subject to stand in some other kind of relation to an object before he can refer to that object. "Being before the mind" might just be a way of designating this other kind of relation that is a precondition for reference without saying anything substantive about the intrinsic nature of this relation. But then Price would not be describing what it is about the nature of consciousness that intelligibly explains why being conscious of an object produces an ability to refer to that object; he would just be noting that consciousness is of such a nature as to intelligibly produce such abilities. So we need to dig deeper if we are to understand what it is about the nature of experience that intelligibly grounds its power to produce abilities to refer.

An experiencing subject is not only conscious of an object but also conscious of observable properties of that object. Moreover, he is conscious of the object in virtue of being conscious of some of its observable properties. (I am visually conscious of the tomato in virtue of being conscious of its redness and roundness.) If we are to understand how a subject's consciousness of an object intelligibly explains his ability to refer to it in thought, then what we need to understand is how a subject's consciousness of observable properties of an object enables him to refer to that object in thought.

I submit that the relevance of consciousness here is that, as we saw in chapter 2, consciousness combines with the observable properties of the object of experience to produce phenomenal properties of the experience. It is because an experience has phenomenal character, a phenomenal character intelligibly determined by properties of the experienced object, that the experience has the intelligible causal power to produce in the subject of the experience an ability to refer to the experienced object. *How* does the phenomenal character intelligibly ground this causal power? As we have seen, phenomenal properties are similar in a certain way to the observable properties that intelligibly determine them (sec. 2.4). Specifically, such phenomenal properties just are observable properties instantiated in a special way. Observable properties are instantiated in two ways in experience: they are instantiated in the standard nonphenomenal way *in* the object of experience, and they are instantiated in a special phenomenal way *for* the subject of the experience. When observable properties are instantiated in the nonphenomenal way, we say simply that we have observable properties being instantiated; when they are instantiated in the phenomenal way, we say we have phenomenal properties being instantiated. This special phenomenal kind of instantiation holds the key to an intelligible explanation of how experiences produce abilities to refer, for the *nature* of this kind of instantiation is such that when properties are instantiated in this way, a subject is enabled to refer to them. More specifically, properties instantiated in this special way are instantiated for a subject in that they are related to a subject in a way that enables the subject to *focus his attention* on them.[15] Reflect, for example, on what it is like to be conscious of instantiations of redness, and you should be able to discern that there is something about the nature of this phenomenal property that intelligibly explains why a subject who is conscious of such instantiations will be able to focus his attention on them.

We need to be precise in specifying the properties to which the subject of an experience will be able to attend. The observable properties of an object of experience will be instantiated in the standard way at some spatial location, but insofar as these properties are also instantiated in the special phenomenal way for a subject, the subject will be able to attend to these standard property instantiations at the relevant spatial location. Note that although it is these observable properties being instantiated in the special phenomenal way that enables the subject to attend to them, what the subject is attending to are the standard non-phenomenal instantiations of these properties, not the special phenomenal instantiations.[16] Thus when I am experiencing my tomato, for example, I am instantiating the property of phenomenal redness: there is something it is like for me to be conscious of the redness of the tomato. But in virtue of instantiating this property, I am able to attend to the redness of the tomato, not to my own phenomenal redness.

As I will explain presently, in virtue of being able to attend to these standard property instantiations, the subject will also be able to attend to the object of experience in which these observable properties are instantiated. Finally, a subject capable of thought who is focusing his attention on an object will also be able to think about that object and refer to that object in his thinking—thinking about an object just is a way of attending to it.[17] So because experiences have phenomenal character, they do have the intelligible causal power to produce abilities to refer.

I am arguing that phenomenal character intelligibly grounds this causal power insofar as it involves a special kind of instantiation. The idea that the intelligibility of causal powers can be explained in terms of the nature of a kind of instantiation is an idea that we should be willing to entertain, for we are already familiar with a kind of intelligible connection between causal powers and instantiation. Recall that even brute causal powers are possessed in virtue of underlying categorical properties. What makes these causal powers brute is that no intelligible explanatory connection exists between such causal powers and their underlying categorical properties; rather, the explanatory connection is mediated by a brute law of nature. But a limited kind of intelligibility figures in the explanation of even brute causal powers. Consider some brute causal power and its underlying categorical property. The connection between such causal power and its underlying categorical property is not intelligible; it can only be discovered empirically. But what is intelligible is that if that categorical property is to explain (even in a brute way) why some object has that causal power, the categorical property must be *instantiated* in the object. Only *instantiated* categorical properties explain causal powers; the mere existence of an uninstantiated categorical property as an abstract entity explains nothing about why concrete objects have causal powers. Something about the nature of instantiation makes it intelligible that a categorical property that is instantiated in an object can help explain why that object has some causal power. Although connections between particular categorical properties and particular causal powers may be brute, there does seem to be an intelligible connection between objects instantiating categorical properties and having any causal powers at all. Now, just as the standard instantiation of categorical properties in an object is an intelligible necessary condition for such object to have any causal powers at all, I am claiming similarly that there is a special phenomenal kind of instantiation of properties for a subject that is an intelligible necessary condition for the subject to have certain particular kinds of causal powers with respect to those properties. If we are willing to accept the first kind of intelligibility, then we should at least be open to the possibility of the second kind of intelligibility, as well.

I am arguing that a subject can attend to observable properties that are instantiated in the standard nonphenomenal way when these observable properties are also instantiated in the special phenomenal way for the subject. I am also arguing that a subject who can attend to these standard property instantiations can also attend to (and thereby refer to) the *object* that instantiates these properties. What is relevant here is that it is not only observable properties of the object of experience that are instantiated in a phenomenal way; it is the object's very "objectness," so to speak, its property of being an (external) object, that is instantiated in this way. Earlier I referred to this property as the property of externality (sec. 2.5). I explained then that when this property of externality is instantiated in a phenomenal way, the instantiated observable properties to which the subject is attending appear to be properties of an external object. Now, what is the identity of this external object that the observable properties appear to be properties of? Suppose that we are concerned with a nonhallucinatory experience. The observable properties *are* properties of an external object (the object of experience), and this fact intelligibly explains why the observable properties *appear* to be properties of an external object (sec. 2.5). So the object that the observable properties appear to be properties of will be the external object that the observable properties *are* properties of, the object of experience. Since these observable properties appear to be the properties of an object, the subject, in attending to these observable property instantiations, can also attend to this object. And given that the object in question just is the object of experience, the subject will have the power to attend to (and refer to) the object of experience.

Consider again my experience of the tomato. We already know that because I am instantiating the property of phenomenal redness, I can attend to the redness of the tomato. But I am also instantiating the property of phenomenal externality: the redness I am attending to appears to be the redness of an external object (more specifically, it appears to be the redness of a tomato). And the redness does not merely appear to me to be the property of *some* external object; it appears to me to be the property of a *particular* external object. The particular object in question is the tomato I am experiencing. So in virtue of attending to the redness of the tomato, I am able to attend to and refer to the tomato itself.

3.3.2   The Experience's Power to Cause the Subject to Attribute Observable Properties

I began this section (3.3) by noting that an experience's intelligible causal power to produce certain kinds of beliefs can be thought of as combining two intelligible causal powers: the power to produce in the subject the ability to refer to the object of experience, and the power to cause the subject to attribute appropriate observable properties to the object of experience. The appropriate observable properties are those that are instantiated by the object of experience. I have now articulated as best as I can the nature of the intelligible connection between the intrinsic nature of experience and the first of these causal powers. Let us now examine the second of these intelligible causal powers of experience. I am assuming that the subject already has the *ability* to attribute the relevant observable properties to objects; my interest is in the experience's power to cause the subject to *exercise* this ability. I allow that the subject can be caused to exercise this ability in both brute and intelligible ways. But, I claim, an *experience* can cause the subject to exercise this ability in an intelligible way.

We are already in a position to understand how the experience enables the subject to exercise this ability in an intelligible way. We have seen that the observable properties of the object of experience intelligibly determine the phenomenal properties of the experience. In turn, these phenomenal properties intelligibly enable the subject to attend to the instantiated observable properties. I now merely need to add that sufficient attention to these observable properties intelligibly results in the subject believing that such properties are instantiated; we can say that the subject *recognizes* that such properties are instantiated, in the sense that his belief is an intelligible response to his attending to those instantiated observable properties. (To say that x is an *intelligible response* to y is just another way of saying that x is intelligibly caused by y. And, of course, to say that x is *intelligibly caused* by y is just to say that x comes about as the result of the exercise of an intelligible causal power of y.) Moreover, insofar as these observable properties appear to be the properties of some object, the subject will intelligibly attribute those properties to that object. (The attribution is intelligible insofar as it is intelligibly caused.)

The idea that sufficient attention to these observable properties intelligibly causes the subject to believe that these properties are instantiated was already implicit in my earlier claim that phenomenal properties reveal the presence of their corresponding observable properties (sec. 2.4). A phenomenal property that corresponds to an observable property just is that observable property instantiated in a special kind of way. The nature of this special kind of instantiation is such as to reveal the presence of the observable property, in the sense that believing that the observable property is present (i.e., instantiated in the standard way) is an intelligible response to the property being instantiated in the special phenomenal kind of way. The intelligibility of the response can better be understood if we see the response as proceeding in two steps. Consider some observable property being instantiated in both the standard nonphenomenal way and the special phenomenal way. We have already seen that the nature of phenomenal instantiation is such as to enable the subject to attend to the standard nonphenomenal instantiations of the property. What I am adding here is that the nature of phenomenal instantiation is also such as to enable the subject to believe that the property is instantiated upon sufficient attention to those property instantiations. How much attention is needed will depend on the determinateness and complexity of the property. Red is not too determinate a color property, and therefore not too much attention is needed to recognize that some object of experience is red. The belief that some object is red follows pretty automatically on the experience of the redness of that object. But maroon is a more determinate color property, and so more attention is needed to intelligibly form the belief that some object of experience is maroon. Regardless, what is important here is that a sufficient amount of attention to an instantiated observable property can intelligibly give rise to a belief that said observable property is instantiated.[18]

3.3.3   The Experience's Power to Cause the Subject to Believe in External Objects

We have distinguished two types of phenomenal properties: phenomenal properties that correspond to observable properties (e.g., phenomenal redness, phenomenal orange) and the property of phenomenal externality, which corresponds to the property of externality. I will refer to properties of the former type as *phenomenal observable properties*. I now claim that just as the instantiation of some phenomenal observable property in a subject's experience can intelligibly cause the subject to believe that the corresponding observable property is instantiated, so too the instantiation of the property of phenomenal externality can intelligibly cause the subject to believe that the property of externality is instantiated. In other words, a subject's perceptual experience can intelligibly cause him to believe that there is an external object present before him. Now, there is an important difference between phenomenal observable properties and the property of phenomenal externality that might suggest an objection to the claim I am now making. Whereas phenomenal observable properties cannot be instantiated without their corresponding observable properties being instantiated, the property of phenomenal externality can be instantiated without the property of externality being instantiated (i.e., in hallucinatory experiences) (sec. 2.5). A phenomenal observable property can be intelligibly explained only by its corresponding observable property, whereas the property of phenomenal externality can be explained by something other than the property of externality. So it might be thought that the instantiation of some phenomenal observable property can intelligibly give rise to the belief that the corresponding observable property is instantiated, because the phenomenal observable property cannot be instantiated without the observable property being instantiated. Whereas, the objector claims, the instantiation of the property of phenomenal externality cannot intelligibly give rise to the belief that the property of externality is instantiated, because the property of phenomenal externality can be instantiated without the property of externality being instantiated.

The objection fails because it misunderstands how phenomenal properties intelligibly give rise to beliefs about corresponding nonphenomenal properties. It mistakenly assumes that such beliefs are acquired through inference to the best explanation. Thus suppose experiences gave rise to beliefs in the following manner. I have an experience in which some phenomenal property is instantiated. I then introspect the experience to be able to attend to the phenomenal property. I attend to it, reflect on its nature, and consider what the best explanation is of that phenomenal property being instantiated. Suppose the phenomenal property I am considering is some phenomenal observable property. I conclude that the phenomenal property can only be explained by the corresponding observable property, and I therefore believe that such observable property is instantiated. Such a belief is intelligibly formed (i.e., intelligibly caused) because my conclusion that the phenomenal property can only be explained by the corresponding observable property is correct. But now suppose that the phenomenal property I am considering is the property of phenomenal externality. And suppose that I similarly conclude that the phenomenal property can only be explained by the property of externality, and I therefore believe that an external object is present before me. My belief would not be intelligibly formed because something other than the property of externality can explain the property of phenomenal externality. So if it had been the case that experiences caused beliefs about nonphenomenal properties in the way just described, the objector would be correct: the instantiation of the property of phenomenal externality could not intelligibly give rise to the belief that the property of externality is instantiated.

Of course, it is not the case that experiences give rise to beliefs about nonphenomenal properties in this indirect, inferential way. I do not need to attend to and consider phenomenal properties to intelligibly form beliefs about nonphenomenal properties; I do not even need to know what phenomenal properties are. The phenomenal properties of an experience intelligibly ground its causal powers to produce beliefs about nonphenomenal properties, but as we have seen, the way they intelligibly ground these causal powers is not by enabling the subject of the experience to attend to the phenomenal properties but by enabling the subject to attend to the nonphenomenal properties. When a phenomenal observable property is instantiated, the subject is enabled to attend to the corresponding observable property, and upon sufficient attention, he intelligibly comes to believe that such observable property is instantiated. The subject does not infer from the phenomenal property to the observable property; on the contrary, he may not be thinking of the phenomenal property at all. His attention is directed in the first instance to the observable property, and therefore he is able to come to believe that it is instantiated.

Now, what can the subject attend to when the property of phenomenal externality is instantiated? Given that what a subject can attend to is intelligibly determined by the phenomenal character of the experience, and given that the phenomenal character of a veridical experience (i.e., a nonhallucinatory experience) can be the same as the phenomenal character of a hallucinatory experience, then what the subject can attend to in virtue of the property of phenomenal externality being instantiated will be the same regardless of whether the experience is veridical or hallucinatory.[19] So the subject cannot attend to the instantiation of the property of externality, for the property of externality is not instantiated in hallucinatory experiences. And the subject, absent introspection (see section 3.6), is not enabled to attend to the property of phenomenal externality, either; as just noted, phenomenal properties intelligibly ground causal powers to produce beliefs about nonphenomenal properties by enabling the subject to attend to nonphenomenal properties, not phenomenal properties. So what are the nonphenomenal properties to which the subject can attend in virtue of the property of phenomenal externality being instantiated? What the subject can attend to are instantiations of observable properties that appear *unified* in a certain way. As I explained in chapter 2 (sec. 2.2), observable properties are instantiated in both veridical and hallucinatory experiences. And as I also explained there (sec. 2.5), these instantiations of observable properties can appear unified in a way that is constituted by the instantiation of the property of phenomenal externality. We can also say that the nature of this unity is such that the observable properties *appear* to the subject to be the properties of an external object. Now, what is the force of the word "appear" here? I suggest that its force is just to convey that the nature of the unity is such that for the subject who is attending to observable properties that appear unified in this way, it is *intelligible* to believe that such observable properties are properties of an external object; it is intelligible to believe that such observable properties are unified *in* and *by* an external object. It is intelligible for the subject to believe it in the sense that such a belief would be intelligibly caused. I have already argued that a subject who sufficiently attends to instantiations of some observable property, and thereby believes that such observable property is instantiated, has a belief that is intelligibly caused (sec. 3.3.2). Similarly, I am now arguing that a subject who is attending to observable properties that appear to be properties of an external object, and who thereupon believes that such observable properties are properties of an external object, also has a belief that is intelligibly caused. Of course, such a belief may be false, for it may be caused by a hallucinatory experience. But there is no reason to think that beliefs that are intelligibly caused cannot be false.

Consider, once more, my experience of the tomato, or if you like, suppose I am visually hallucinating a tomato; it doesn't matter. Either way, I will be attending to instantiations of the property of redness. But I am not attending merely to multiple instantiations of the property of redness spread out in space; I am attending to multiple instantiations of the property of redness that appear in a certain way; they appear to be unified in an external object, a tomato. I thereupon believe that there is an external object before me (a tomato). Moreover, given the way the redness appears to me, it *makes sense*, it is *intelligible*, that I form this belief; the belief is not a brute, arbitrary response to the experience but an intelligible response to it. Which is just to say that my experience has the power to intelligibly cause me to form this belief.

In chapter 4, I explain how the fact that our experiences *intelligibly* cause us to believe that external objects exist enables us to show that, contrary to the skeptic's claims, we are *justified* in believing that external objects exist.

3.4   The Intelligible Causal Powers of Beliefs: Inference

Let us turn to another way in which beliefs can intelligibly be caused. Beliefs can be caused by experiences, but they can also be caused by other kinds of mental states. In particular, beliefs can be caused by other beliefs via the process of inference. In this section I argue that some cases of inference are instances of intelligible causation. Beliefs, as well as experiences, have intelligible causal powers.

Consider a case of valid deductive inference: a subject's belief that p causes him to believe that q, where q is a necessary consequence of p. Is the subject's belief that q intelligibly caused? If the belief that q is intelligibly caused, it is because the belief that p has the intelligible causal power to produce the belief that q. The causal power of the belief that p to produce the belief that q is an intelligible causal power if it is intelligibly connected to its underlying categorical property. Is there anything about the intrinsic categorical nature of a belief that would intelligibly ground such a causal power?

Let us suppose that the belief that p is conscious when it causes the belief that q. What is the intrinsic categorical nature of a conscious belief? Conscious mental states are states that include acts of consciousness. Whereas a nonhallucinatory experience involves an act of consciousness directed toward a concrete object, a belief, being a propositional attitude, involves an act of consciousness directed toward a propositional object. Moreover, insofar as the belief is a propositional *attitude*, the act of consciousness will be in the form of a determinate attitude toward the proposition. Specifically, the determinate attitude with which a believer is conscious of a proposition is that he holds the proposition to be true.

Conscious states also have what-it-is-like properties (i.e., phenomenal properties). Acts of consciousness always combine with the objects of those acts to produce phenomenal properties that are intelligibly determined by the properties of those objects. Moreover, the phenomenal character of a conscious state always enables the subject to attend to and reflect on the object of consciousness (sec. 3.3). The subject who consciously believes a proposition p is able to attend to and reflect on p.

In particular, such a subject intelligibly has the power to reflect on the question of whether q is a necessary consequence of p (assuming that he understands what a necessary consequence is). Of course, it does not follow that he has the power to find the answer to this question; whether he does so might depend on the quality of his intelligence. The subject might not be intelligent enough to determine whether p entails q. But suppose he is intelligent enough, and as a result of reflection, he concludes that p does entail q; he forms the conscious *belief* that p entails q. We now have a subject who consciously believes both p and (p entails q). I claim that such a subject does have the intelligible causal power to come to believe q. Something about the intrinsic nature of simultaneously holding these two beliefs intelligibly grounds such a causal power. The subject consciously believes p and thereby holds p to be true. He simultaneously holds it to be true that p entails q: if p is true, then q must be true. Given that the subject holds p to be true, he can intelligibly come to believe (hold to be true) that the antecedent of the aforementioned conditional is true. (To say that a subject *intelligibly* comes to believe something is to say that he comes to believe it as the result of the exercise of an intelligible causal power.) And given that he holds the conditional itself to be true, he can intelligibly come to believe that the consequent of this conditional is true, as well (for the intrinsic nature of holding a conditional to be true is such that if one simultaneously holds the antecedent to be true, then it is intelligible that one can come to hold true the consequent, as well). In other words, the subject can intelligibly come to believe q. So a subject who does consciously and simultaneously believe both p and (p entails q) does have the intelligible causal power to infer that q.

Perhaps some will object that just as a lack of sufficient intelligence can prevent a subject who consciously believes p from having causal powers to acquire beliefs in certain necessary consequences of p, so too a sufficient lack of intelligence could perhaps also prevent a subject who consciously believes both p and (p entails q) from having the causal power to acquire the belief that q.[20] But the force of my argument is that it is the intrinsic nature of the aforementioned two beliefs that intelligibly confers the causal power in question; to have the causal power in question, the subject does not need any intelligence in addition to the intelligence needed to have the beliefs in the first place. Of course, the subject *will* require some intelligence to have the beliefs in the first place; a subject cannot consciously believe that p entails q, for example, unless he consciously grasps the idea of entailment (i.e., necessary consequence), and to do so presumably requires some cognitive sophistication. But given that the subject has the two conscious beliefs, and thereby has the intelligence required to have the two beliefs, the subject requires no additional intelligence to have the causal power to acquire the belief that q. The intrinsic natures of consciously believing p (holding p to be true in a conscious way) and consciously believing that p entails q (holding it to be true in a conscious way that if p is true, then q must be true) intelligibly confer on the subject the causal power in question.

Someone might wish to point out that sometimes the intelligible response to believing p and believing that p entails q is to give up the belief that p (or to give up the belief that p entails q) rather than acquiring the belief that q.[21] I agree. In arguing that a subject who consciously believes both p and (p entails q) has the intelligible causal power to acquire the belief that q, I implicitly assumed that the subject had no other relevant conscious mental states. If we instead assume that the subject does have other relevant conscious mental states (e.g., a conscious belief that not q), then things become more complicated. Depending on other relevant factors, the subject in such a situation might have both the intelligible power to acquire the belief that q and the intelligible power to give up the belief that p,[22] or he might have only one of these powers. We need not enter into these complications here. My point is merely that if a subject, for whatever reason or for no reason, consciously holds some proposition p to be true, and if that subject also holds it to be true that if such proposition p is true, then some other proposition q must be true, as well, then absent any other relevant factors, it is intelligible for the subject to hold q to be true. My aim here is not to give a complete theory of the conditions under which subjects have various intelligible causal powers. I aim only to show that beliefs, like experiences, do have intelligible causal powers, and that beliefs acquired by inference are sometimes intelligibly caused.

3.5 The Intelligible Causal Powers of Rational Intuitions: Reflection

Think back to our subject consciously attending to p and reflecting on the question of whether p entails q. He reaches the conclusion that p entails q, and he comes to believe that p entails q. Is our subject's belief intelligibly caused? It depends on how it was formed. If the belief just pops into the subject's head, in the sense that it was not caused by some prior conscious state, then the belief was not intelligibly caused. Only conscious mental states can be intelligible causes (sec. 3.1). But many times a belief formed by reflection will be caused by a prior conscious state. We are all familiar with the process of consciously reflecting on a question for a while and suddenly seeming to *see* the answer: all of a sudden, we seem to see that some proposition p does indeed entail a certain proposition q. The fact that p entails q seems to *reveal* itself to us, and therefore we can *see* it. And since we see that p entails q, we then believe (hold it to be true) that p entails q. The belief does not just pop into one's head; rather, it seems to be an intelligible response to the seeing. I claim that many beliefs produced by reflection are intelligibly caused by such seeings.

Of course, we literally see only with our eyes, so we do not literally see that logical relations obtain. Nevertheless we talk of "seeing" here because of the similarities between such conscious states and perceptual experiences. Philosophers have traditionally referred to such conscious states as rational intuitions; one (rationally) intuits that p entails q.[23] Rational intuitions are similar to experiences with respect to the nature of their phenomenal properties. As we have seen, phenomenal properties always correspond to certain nonphenomenal properties; the phenomenal properties just are the nonphenomenal properties instantiated in a special phenomenal way (sec. 2.4). The nonphenomenal properties that correspond to the phenomenal properties of a conscious belief are representational properties. Beliefs are attitudes to propositions, and propositions are by their nature representational entities. Thus the phenomenal character of a conscious belief that p will include the phenomenal instantiation of the property of representing p. More precisely, the phenomenal character of this conscious belief will just be the phenomenal instantiation of the property of holding the representation of p to be true. But whereas the phenomenal properties of beliefs correspond to representational properties (and properties of having attitudes to representations), the phenomenal properties of experiences correspond to both representational properties and nonrepresentational properties (sec. 2.3). Rational intuitions are similar to experiences in that there are also phenomenal properties of rational intuitions that correspond to nonrepresentational properties. Whereas the nonrepresentational properties that correspond to the phenomenal properties of experiences are the observable properties of concrete external objects and the observable (spatial) relations that hold between them, the nonrepresentational properties that correspond to the phenomenal properties of rational intuitions are the logical and other necessary relations that hold between abstract objects. When I consciously *believe* that p entails q, it is my representing that p entails q that is instantiated in the special phenomenal way. But when I consciously *intuit* that p entails q, it is the relation of entailment itself, not my representing it, that is instantiated in the special phenomenal way. Of course, relations are instantiated by *obtaining* between relata. So we can say that when I intuit that p entails q, the relation of entailment obtains between p and q in the special phenomenal way.

Previously I argued that beliefs about the observable properties of external objects are intelligible responses to experiences of such properties, because the phenomenal character of these experiences is such as to enable the subject to attend to the instantiations of these observable properties (sec. 3.3). Similarly, beliefs that logical relations obtain between propositions are intelligible responses to rational intuitions of such logical relations obtaining between propositions, because the phenomenal character of these intuitions is such as to enable the subject to attend to the logical relations obtaining between the propositions. Consciousness not only reveals the external, concrete world to us but also reveals the world of abstract objects to us.[24]

3.6   Intelligible Causation and Introspection

We have seen that conscious mental states have intelligible causal powers to produce beliefs in virtue of their phenomenal properties. Specifically, a conscious mental state with some phenomenal property has the intelligible causal power to produce the belief that the corresponding nonphenomenal property is instantiated. In the case of (perceptual) experiences, the nonphenomenal properties corresponding to the phenomenal properties of experiences include observable properties of external objects. So the beliefs intelligibly produced by experiences will include perceptual beliefs. But typically the nonphenomenal properties corresponding to the phenomenal properties of conscious mental states will merely be properties of those states; in other words, they will be mental properties. When conscious mental states intelligibly produce beliefs that such mental properties are instantiated, the beliefs are appropriately characterized as introspective beliefs. So perceptual beliefs and introspective beliefs can be produced in the same way: they can intelligibly be caused by conscious mental states in virtue of their phenomenal properties. Introspection does not require a process that is similar to, but distinct from, the process that produces perceptual beliefs. One does not have to "look inward," say, to acquire introspective knowledge. Perceptual and introspective beliefs can be produced by the same process; they differ only in their content.

Consider the example of experiences again. When discussing the phenomenal properties of experiences, I focused for the most part on how they are intelligibly related to the observable properties of external objects. But there are also phenomenal properties of experiences that are intelligibly related to the representational properties of the underlying acts of consciousness (sec. 2.2, 2.3). Therefore experiences can intelligibly produce both beliefs that observable properties are instantiated and beliefs that representational properties are instantiated. The former beliefs are perceptual, the latter are introspective, but they are all formed in the same way. When I experience a red object, for example, the phenomenal character of the experience includes both a phenomenal property that corresponds to the property of redness (phenomenal redness) and a phenomenal property that corresponds to the property of representing redness. Therefore I can intelligibly come to believe both that there is a red object before me and that I am representing that object as red. The former belief is perceptual, the latter is introspective, but both beliefs are intelligibly caused by the experience in virtue of phenomenal properties of the experience.

Experiences are not the only conscious mental states that can intelligibly give rise to introspective beliefs; all conscious mental states can do so. Earlier we talked about the nature of conscious beliefs (sec. 3.4). The phenomenal character of the conscious belief that p corresponds to the nonphenomenal property of holding the representation of p to be true. So when I consciously believe that p, I can intelligibly form the second-order belief that I believe p, that is, that I hold p to be true. I typically will not have any need to form such beliefs about my beliefs, but I can do so, and I can do so intelligibly. And the way that I can do so is no different from the way in which I form perceptual beliefs in response to my experiences.

Let me slightly qualify my claim that introspective beliefs and perceptual beliefs are produced by the same kind of process.

Introspective beliefs about nonphenomenal properties of mental states are produced in the same way that perceptual beliefs are produced. But introspective beliefs about phenomenal properties are produced in a somewhat different way. So far I have argued that phenomenal properties intelligibly ground causal powers to produce beliefs that their corresponding nonphenomenal properties are instantiated. I now wish to claim that phenomenal properties also intelligibly ground causal powers to produce beliefs that these very phenomenal properties are themselves instantiated. When I have an experience of red, not only can I intelligibly come to believe, say, that there is a red object before me, but I can also intelligibly come to believe that my experience instantiates the property of phenomenal redness. But the process by which I come to acquire this latter belief is somewhat different from the process by which I come to have the former belief. Although I come to have beliefs about nonphenomenal properties by means of phenomenal properties that correspond to them, I do not come to have beliefs about these phenomenal properties by means of an additional level of phenomenal properties that correspond to *them*. There are no second-level phenomenal properties that correspond to first-level phenomenal properties, for we do not have experiences of our experiences (or of any of our other conscious mental states) in the way we have experiences of external objects.[25] Rather, the unique nature of phenomenal properties is such that we can intelligibly come to detect their presence without the mediation of an additional level of phenomenal character.

But how are we able to do so? It is difficult to be precise here. Recall that the phenomenal properties of experience enable us to believe that corresponding observable properties are instantiated by enabling us to *attend* to instantiations of those observable properties (sec. 3.3). Similarly, I think that when we succeed in intelligibly forming beliefs that the phenomenal properties themselves are instantiated, it is because we succeed in attending to *their* instantiations. Somehow, though, it is more difficult to attend to (instantiations of) phenomenal properties than it is to attend to observable properties. For example, it seems to be more difficult for me to attend to what it is like for me to be conscious of redness than it is for me to attend to the redness itself. Attention seems to be naturally focused on the external world; turning it inward on oneself seems to require more effort. Also, attending to phenomenal properties seems to be difficult because it seems to require that one's attention operate simultaneously at two distinct levels: it seems that I cannot attend to what it is like for me to be conscious of redness without also simultaneously attending to the redness. Moreover, the difficulty of attending to phenomenal properties is such that it seems that one can attend to them for only very short periods of time. I can sit in front of an apple tree and focus my attention on the striking redness of an apple continuously for a half hour or even longer. But I cannot focus my attention on what it is like for me to be conscious of that redness for a similarly long period of time; rather, I seem to grasp the what-it-is-like property for only moments, and then my attention seems to "drop down" to the redness itself. Thus phenomenal character is elusive; our knowledge of phenomenal character constantly needs to be replenished and reinforced by ever new attentions.[26]

But despite the difficulty of attending to phenomenal properties, we can succeed in doing so, and we can succeed in intelligibly forming beliefs about the instantiation and nature of these phenomenal properties. As I have noted many times, the underlying idea of this inquiry is that we can discover the intelligible

features of conscious states by reflecting on the intrinsic features of conscious states made known to us through introspection (sec. 1.1, 1.3, 2.1). Among the central intrinsic features of
conscious states are phenomenal properties. And the way phenomenal properties are "made known to us by introspection" is
through attending to them. If my claims here about phenomenal properties are correct, it is because I have succeeded in sufficiently attending to phenomenal properties. If you, my reader,
wish to evaluate my claims, you need to sufficiently attend to
them, as well. I hope that you make the effort.

4   The Importance of Consciousness I: Belief, Rationality, and Knowledge

4.1   Consciousness and Rationality

We are not merely conscious beings; we are also rational beings. That consciousness is a part of our lives is a wonderful thing, and it is even more of a wonder that we are privileged to enjoy both consciousness and rationality in our lives. But these two phenomena are not unrelated. Consciousness is required for rationality; we cannot exercise our rationality in the absence of conscious mental states. In this chapter, I explain how consciousness enables us to be rational; I also explain how consciousness makes possible another related phenomenon of supreme importance in our lives: our possession of knowledge.

We are conscious beings insofar as we have conscious mental states, and we are rational beings insofar as we are able to exercise our rationality in the production of rational mental states. But what is it that makes a mental state rational? More fundamentally, what is it about mental states that makes them characterizable in terms of rationality and irrationality in the first place? The states of a washing machine or a potted plant, for example, are simply not the sort of thing that can be rational *or* irrational; only mental states are appropriately characterized in

these terms. But not all mental states are appropriately characterized in these terms. Experiences are either veridical or non-
veridical; they cannot, in addition, be rational or irrational. But
beliefs, unlike experiences, can be rational or irrational (in addition to being true or false). What is it about beliefs that makes
them evaluable in these terms?

Beliefs can be rational or irrational whereas experiences cannot, because beliefs, but not experiences, are propositional attitudes. As we have seen, to believe that p is to hold a certain
kind of attitude toward the proposition p (sec. 3.4); specifically,
one who believes p holds p to be true or, equivalently, regards p
as true. Some (but not all) propositional attitudes can be evaluated with respect to rationality because certain kinds of attitudes
toward propositions can be evaluated with respect to rationality;
it is attitudes toward propositions, not propositions themselves,
that are rational or irrational. An attitude can be evaluated with
respect to rationality insofar as a question can arise as to whether
the attitude is *appropriate* in a certain kind of way. If the attitude
is appropriate in the relevant sense, it is rational; otherwise it is
irrational. Rationality is a kind of appropriateness that pertains
to attitudes toward propositions.

What kind of appropriateness is involved here? I do not have
a general theory at hand, but let us continue to focus on the
case of beliefs. Suppose I believe p: I regard p as being true. Now,
whether p is in fact true will typically not be up to me; the truth
of p may have nothing to do with me. Whether p is true is a
matter of whether the world is the way p represents it to be, and
whether the world is that way is a fact about the world, and not,
typically, a fact about myself. But given that it is not up to me
as to whether p is true, we may wonder whether it is appropriate
for me to regard p as being true. With what "right" do I regard p

as being true, if p's being true has nothing to do with me? Presumably if it is appropriate for me to hold this attitude toward p, other facts about me must make it appropriate for me to hold this attitude toward p. These additional facts must make it *rational* for me to regard p as being true; they must, if you like, give me a *reason* for thinking that p is true. It is sometimes said that the rationality of a belief must be connected with the possibility of that belief being true;[1] I agree. The rationality of a belief is connected with its truth because belief itself is connected with truth: to believe p is to regard p as true, and therefore to rationally believe p is to *appropriately* regard p as true.

What role does consciousness play in our ability to have rational beliefs and rational propositional attitudes of other kinds? One way consciousness is relevant here is that only conscious propositional attitudes can be rational. Strictly speaking, beliefs and other propositional attitudes must be conscious mental states, for the different attitudes we can take toward propositions are just determinate ways we can be conscious of propositions.[2] Conscious propositional attitudes involve acts of consciousness directed toward propositions; the acts of consciousness are instantiated in the form of determinate kinds of attitudes toward such propositions (sec. 3.4). Thus when I believe that p, say, the way I am conscious of the proposition p is that I regard it as being true; regarding a proposition as true is just a way of being conscious of it. Regarding-as-true and other attitude properties are properties of acts of consciousness. So we already see one sense in which consciousness is required for rationality. We are rational when we have appropriate attitudes toward propositions, and it is only when we are in conscious states that we stand in attitudes toward propositions.

But when I began this chapter by claiming that consciousness is required for rationality, I had a more substantive claim
in mind. Specifically, not only must rational states *be* conscious
states, but other conscious states are required to *make* these
states rational. As we have seen, for a propositional attitude to be
rational is for it to be held in a certain kind of appropriate way.
I submit that an attitude is held in the appropriate way if and
only if it is caused in an intelligible way, that is, if and only if it
is intelligibly caused. Since only conscious states can be intelligible causes (sec. 1.1, 3.1), conscious states are required to make
propositional attitudes rational.

Why do I hold that an attitude is held in a rational or appropriate way if and only if it is caused in an intelligible way?
Because there does seem to be a connection between the notion
of appropriateness that we are working with here and the idea
of intelligibility that we have been working with all along. I
am suggesting that rationality just is the idea of intelligibility
as applied to propositional attitudes. Consider, again, the idea
of intelligibility. A cause is intelligible insofar as it involves the
exercise of an intelligible causal power, a causal power that is
intelligibly related to its underlying categorical properties. The
relation is intelligible in that there is something about it that
enables it to be known a priori (sec. 1.1, 3.1). We might say that
it *makes sense* that a state with *those* categorical properties should
have the causal power in question (and therefore our reason can
know this); the causal power flows in an intelligible way (in a
way that makes sense) from those categorical properties. Now,
causal powers are powers to produce certain effects. So when an
intelligible causal power is exercised and produces its effect, an
intelligible connection exists between the cause and the effect.
Given the intrinsic nature of the cause, it is intelligible (it makes

sense) that it produced *that* effect. The effect itself can be said to make sense, in that it makes sense that it occurred, given the intrinsic nature of its cause. Let us turn now to the rationality of propositional attitudes, and let us again focus on beliefs. I have suggested that the question of whether a subject's belief that p is rational is the question of whether it is appropriate for the subject to regard p as true, given that whether p is true is not up to the subject. I now suggest that the question of whether it is appropriate to regard p as true is just the question of whether it makes sense to regard p as true. But it can make sense to be in a state only if there are other states to *make sense* of it, so to speak, and the way other states can make sense of it is by causing it to occur in an intelligible way (in a way that makes sense). If I have been intelligibly caused to regard p as true, then given the nature of that cause, it does make sense that I am regarding p as true (despite it not being up to me whether p is true); in other words, it is appropriate and rational that I regard p as true. Rational propositional attitudes are attitudes that have been intelligibly caused, for attitudes that are intelligibly caused are appropriately held.[3]

In the previous chapter, we looked at various ways in which beliefs can be intelligibly caused. Perceptual beliefs can be intelligibly caused by experiences, beliefs about necessary relations can be intelligibly caused by rational intuitions, introspective beliefs can be intelligibly caused by a variety of conscious mental states, and an inferential belief that q can be intelligibly caused jointly by the conscious belief that p and the conscious belief that p entails q. We now see that the beliefs in question are not only intelligibly caused but also rationally held. In the previous chapter, I attempted to articulate the nature of the intelligible connections that hold between these beliefs and their causes.

We now see that in so doing, I was at the same time attempting to articulate why it is rational (appropriate) to hold such beliefs. Not only does consciousness enable us to take up attitudes toward the world of propositions, but it also enables us to hold these attitudes in rational ways.

4.2   Rationality and Reasoning

Some philosophers seem to want to equate rationality with a capacity for reasoning. They are thinking of reasoning as the process of inference, the process of forming new beliefs that are inferentially related to one's old beliefs. (As my topic in this chapter is the rationality of beliefs, I am concerned here with theoretical reasoning only. I briefly discuss practical reasoning in section 2 of chapter 5.) A rational belief will then be a belief that is formed as the result of "sufficiently good" reasoning. Presumably the goodness of the reasoning will be reflected in the relations between the propositional contents of the newly formed belief and the old beliefs. So according to this view, a rational belief can be thought of as a belief that stands in "rational relations" to other beliefs, where rational relations just are the sort of relations that result from sufficiently good reasoning.[4]

The difficulty with this view is that it gives us no guidance as to what should count as sufficiently good reasoning, or what kinds of relations should count as rational relations. Philosophers who hold that rational beliefs are beliefs that stand in rational relations to other beliefs are committed to the view that only inferential beliefs can be rational; such philosophers typically say that a belief is rational only if it coheres sufficiently with other beliefs. But it is notoriously difficult to give an account of coherence.[5] Should coherence be understood narrowly to include only relations of (deductive) logical consequence, or should it be understood broadly to require only relations of mere logical consistency? Or should it be understood in some intermediate way, as allowing inductive, explanatory, and evidential relations in addition to relations of deductive consequence? And how do we even go about answering this question? Moreover, even if we could answer this question, how would we decide how much coherence is *sufficient* coherence: how much coherence does it take for a belief to be rational? The view that a rational belief is a belief produced by sufficiently good reasoning fails to give us any guidance about what good reasoning is because it fails to specify a *goal* for reasoning. If reasoning had a goal, then presumably good reasoning would be reasoning that met that goal. But if reasoning does not have a goal, then it becomes unclear not only what good reasoning is but why we should care about it or about the notion of rationality that is defined in terms of it.

In my view of rationality, it *is* clear why we care about having rational beliefs: rational beliefs are beliefs that are appropriately held, and we care about holding our beliefs appropriately. When we reflect on the intrinsic nature of acts of conscious believing, we realize that philosophical talk about propositional attitudes is not mere metaphor, for when we consciously believe a proposition, we literally take an attitude toward that proposition: we consciously regard it as true. As I explained earlier, regarding a proposition as true can be appropriate or inappropriate, and if we are going to bother taking attitudes toward propositions, we presumably have some interest in our attitudes being appropriate. Reasoning is important to us insofar as it can produce beliefs that are appropriately held, and good reasoning (that is, *rational* reasoning) can be defined as reasoning that produces beliefs that are appropriately held (i.e., rational beliefs). It is the notion of rationality that should define good reasoning, not vice versa. But once we see that rationality, not reasoning (i.e., inference), is the primary notion here, then we have no reason to think that only inferential beliefs can be rational. A noninferential perceptual belief intelligibly caused by an experience is no less rational than an inferential belief intelligibly caused by other beliefs. Reasoning is important to us because it can produce beliefs in an intelligible way, but as we saw in chapter 3, it is not the only process that can produce beliefs in an intelligible way.

4.3   Some Applications of the Theory of Rationality

Another advantage of my account of rationality is that it helps to illuminate what is at stake in some of the long-standing philosophical debates about rationality. So, for example, ever since Hume, philosophers have argued about whether inductive inference is rational.[6] I suggest that what is really at issue in this debate is whether beliefs produced by inductive inference are intelligibly caused (for rational beliefs are beliefs that are intelligibly caused). Consider some seemingly legitimate inductive argument. There are a hundred premises, each premise consisting of an observation of some distinct a that it is F. (If you don't think a hundred premises are sufficient to produce a seemingly valid inductive argument, then substitute whatever number of premises you think would be sufficient. And add whatever premises are necessary to establish that the observed a's are a sufficiently representative sample.) The inductive conclusion is that (probably) all a's are F. Now consider a subject who consciously believes each of the one hundred premises and also consciously believes that each of the one hundred premises is an instance of the general claim that all a's are F. The subject then consciously infers to the conclusion that all a's are F; he acquires the conscious belief that all a's are F. The question of whether the subject's inference is rational is just the question of whether the subject's newly formed belief that all a's are F is intelligibly caused jointly by his belief that each of the one hundred a's is F, and by his belief that each of the one hundred a's being F is an instance of the general claim that all a's are F. This question is admittedly a difficult one to answer, so it is no wonder that philosophers have not agreed on the question of whether induction is rational. On the one hand, the causation here seems to be different from paradigm instances of thoughts being brutely caused; the subject's belief that all a's are F does not seem to be brutely caused, for example, in the way that the thoughts about monsters I have while sleeping are brutely caused by my indigestion. On the other hand, the subject's belief is not *clearly* intelligibly caused in the way that some inferential beliefs are clearly intelligibly caused. As I explained in the previous chapter (sec. 3.4), if a subject believes that p (regards p as true), and believes that p entails q (regards it as true that if p is true, then q must be true), then clearly it is intelligible for the subject to regard q as true. But it is at least not obvious that a subject who regards it as true that there are one hundred a's that are F should also find it intelligible to regard as true the claim that (probably) all a's are F. I do not know how to resolve this question about the rationality of induction.[7] My only point here is that if one is going to argue that induction is rational, then one needs to argue that beliefs formed by inductive inference are intelligibly caused, in the way that I argued in the previous chapter that various kinds of beliefs, both inferential and noninferential, are intelligibly caused.[8]

Although I do not know how to employ my account of rationality to answer every outstanding question about rationality, I do know how to employ it to answer some of these questions. Consider a lottery with a million tickets, each with an equal chance to win. I submit that it is not rational for John to believe that his ticket will lose, for John's beliefs about the lottery (there are a million tickets; each has an equal chance to win; I, John, have a ticket) do not jointly have the power to intelligibly cause him to believe that his ticket will lose. The best way to see this is to note that John's beliefs do have the intelligible power to produce in him a different belief, the belief that there is a 99.9999 percent chance that his ticket will lose. His beliefs also have the intelligible power to produce in him the belief that his ticket will most probably lose. But if John's beliefs can intelligibly produce beliefs in these probabilistic claims, then they cannot also intelligibly produce the belief in the unqualified claim that his ticket will lose. If these beliefs make it intelligible for John to regard it as true that his ticket will *most probably* lose, then they cannot also make it intelligible for him simply to drop the probabilistic qualification and regard it as true that his ticket *will* lose.

My account of rationality also enables me to respond to the external-world skeptic.[9] In the previous chapter, I argued that a subject's experience has the intelligible power to cause him to believe that external objects exist (sec. 3.3). Thus in response to the skeptic who claims that it is not rational to believe in external objects, I respond that such beliefs are rational insofar as they are intelligibly caused by our experiences. Note how our beliefs that external objects exist differ from John's belief that his lottery ticket will lose. We were able to see that it was not rational for John to believe that his lottery ticket will lose because it was rational for John to believe the "weaker" claim that there is a 99.9999 percent chance that his lottery ticket will lose. But when a subject has a perceptual experience, there is no comparable probabilistic claim that it would be rational for the subject to believe with respect to the existence of external objects. Probabilities just cannot gain a foothold here. As I explained in chapter 3, an experience has the intelligible causal power to produce the belief that an external object exists in virtue of the fact that it instantiates the property of phenomenal externality. It is true that the property of phenomenal externality can be instantiated in the absence of there being an external object present to the subject. But I argued that nevertheless, the nature of phenomenal externality is such that the intelligible response to its instantiation is to believe that there is an external object present. It can be intelligible (and therefore appropriate) to hold some proposition to be true even when it is possibly false. Again, matters would be different if there were some relevant probabilistic claim that it was intelligible to believe here. But there is no such probabilistic claim that it is intelligible to believe here. The nature of phenomenal externality is such that it is not intelligible to respond to its instantiation by, say, believing that there is a 75 percent chance that there is an external object present, or even by believing that it is likely that there is an external object present. Such probabilistic concepts are just not applicable here. More generally, when it is rational for us to believe probabilistic claims, then rationality will prevent us from believing anything more than probabilistic claims. But when it is not rational for us to hold probabilistic beliefs, it may nevertheless be rational for us to believe unqualified "nonprobabilistic" claims about the world. Specifically, it is rational to believe that the world contains external objects, for such beliefs are made rational by our experiences.

So it is rational to believe that some particular external object exists if I perceive it. Is it rational to believe that some external object exists if I see the object on TV or on a movie screen? Is it rational to believe some proposition about the external world if I read in a newspaper that the proposition is true, or if someone tells me that it is true? I am uncertain about the answers to these questions, but I hope that I have at least given some guidance as to how to go about trying to answer them. Presumably such beliefs will be rational if the way they are caused is sufficiently similar to the way beliefs about what we perceive are intelligibly caused by our perceptual experiences. But we should not think that we need to establish that all such beliefs are rational if we are to vindicate our everyday practices. If I am lost and ask a stranger for directions, and he gives me directions and I follow them, we need not suppose that I rationally *believe* what the stranger told me to make sense of my subsequent behavior. *Perhaps* I believe what the stranger told me, but I think it is more likely that I merely *tentatively accept* what the stranger told me, and I act on the basis of this tentative acceptance.[10] I tentatively accept what the stranger told me because I have no rational alternative. Rational beliefs are important to us, but we should not overstate their importance. There are propositional attitudes other than beliefs, and sometimes one of these other propositional attitudes will suffice for our purposes.

Of course, tentative acceptances will presumably have their own standards of appropriateness that they must meet if they are to qualify as rational; I will not address those here. My purpose in this section has merely been to elucidate further my account of rationality by showing the relevance of my account to certain philosophical issues about rationality.

4.4   Two Kinds of Rationality

In the realm of rationality, believing that something is rational can sometimes make it so. Consider again the question of the rationality of induction. Suppose that despite the philosophical controversy that surrounds this issue, Jill believes that at least some instances of inductive inference are rational. In particular, she believes of some one hundred *a*'s that they are *F*, and she also believes that these one hundred *a*'s being *F* makes it rational for her to believe that all *a*'s are *F*. I submit that in this case it is rational (i.e., appropriate) for Jill to believe that all *a*'s are *F*. Given that Jill believes (regards it as *true*) that there are one hundred *a*'s that are *F*, and given that she believes that the one hundred *a*'s being *F* makes it rational for her to believe that all *a*'s are *F*, then surely it is rational and appropriate for her to act on these beliefs and acquire the further belief that all *a*'s are *F*.

Jill's inference is relevantly similar to other cases of inference that we have already characterized as rational. A subject who believes both p and (p entails q) can rationally believe q (sec. 3.4, 4.2). Similarly, the case of Jill suggests that a subject who believes both p and (p entails [it is rational to believe q]) can also rationally believe q. We are willing to allow that the deductive inference is rational, and we should be willing to allow that Jill's quasi-deductive inference is rational, also.

Perhaps some will still be uncomfortable with the fact that Jill's mere belief that her inductive inference is rational can make it so. But we have allowed that a subject's (mere) belief that p entails q can make it rational for the subject to infer q from p, and surely we were right to do so. Regardless of whether it is true that p entails q, so long as the subject *regards* it as true that p entails q, the subject believes rationally when he believes q on the basis of p. Mistaken reasoning can nevertheless be rational reasoning, and similar remarks apply to Jill's reasoning.

In endorsing Jill's reasoning as rational, I am not claiming that reasoning governed by wishful thinking is rational. Jill infers to her inductive conclusion because she truly *believes* that inductive inference is rational, not because she *wishes* or *desires* that it be rational. Belief and desire are different kinds of propositional attitudes, and I am not claiming that it is rational to believe an inductive conclusion based on a mere desire that it be true that inductive inference is rational. But if one actually *believes*, that is, *regards it as true* that inductive inference is rational, then it does seem appropriate that one should act in accordance with one's belief and make inductive inferences.

Thus we should comfortably acknowledge that Jill's belief that all a's are F is a rational and appropriately held belief. Insofar as we still do feel uncomfortable here, I suspect it is because we have a different notion of rationality in mind. There are two different notions of rationality at play here because we possess two different notions of what it takes to hold a belief in an appropriate way. According to the notion of appropriateness I have been developing, a belief is appropriately held if it is intelligibly caused, period. No other conditions are required for the belief to be appropriately held; in particular, the intelligible causes of the belief need not themselves be intelligibly caused. But we also possess a more demanding notion of appropriateness. According to this second notion of appropriateness, in order for a belief to be appropriately held, not only must it be intelligibly caused, but all its causes, both direct and remote, for which a question of appropriateness arises must themselves be intelligibly caused. Whether a question of appropriateness arises for a mental state depends on the kind of mental state it is; specifically, questions of appropriateness arise for certain kinds of propositional attitudes (sec. 4.1). For our purposes, we may simply note that questions of appropriateness arise for beliefs, but not for experiences and rational intuitions. So according to this second notion of appropriateness, an inferential belief will be appropriately held if it is intelligibly caused, and if all beliefs in the causal chain of inference are themselves intelligibly caused. In other words, according to this second notion of appropriateness, an inferential belief can be appropriately held only if all the beliefs from which it is inferred are themselves appropriately held.

For obvious reasons, we might characterize the first notion of appropriateness as *local* appropriateness (and correspondingly, we might talk of local rationality) and the second notion of appropriateness as *global* appropriateness (correspondingly, global rationality). Insofar as we remain uncomfortable about Jill's belief that all a's are F, I think it is because her belief, although locally rational, might be globally irrational. Her belief that all a's are F *will* be globally irrational if one of the causes of her belief, the belief that the one hundred a's being F makes it rational for her to believe that all a's are F, is itself irrational (locally or globally). This latter belief will be irrational if it is inappropriately held, and it is inappropriately held if it is not intelligibly caused. Given the difficulty in showing that induction is rational, we might be inclined to believe that this belief of Jill's is not intelligibly caused. So assume that Jill's belief that all a's are F is locally rational but globally irrational: is her belief rational *simpliciter*? I believe that this question is ill formed. The two notions of rationality are not competing accounts for the correct theory of rationality. Rather, both notions are "correct" in that both describe notions of appropriateness that are genuinely applicable to beliefs. There is more than one way that a belief can be appropriately held.[11]

I have focused so far on local appropriateness, and I hope that it is reasonably clear how a belief being locally appropriate does make it the case that the belief is genuinely held in an appropriate way. Remember how the question of appropriateness arises for beliefs: to believe a proposition is to regard it as being true, and so the question can arise as to whether it is appropriate for a subject to regard some proposition as being true, given that the proposition's being true or false is not something that is typically under the control of the subject. One way of answering this question is to say that what propositions it is appropriate for a subject to regard as true will be a function of what other propositions the subject already regards as true. For example, if a subject already regards some proposition p as true, and also regards it as true that p entails q (if p is true, q must be true), then it is appropriate for the subject to regard q as true, also. According to this way of thinking about appropriateness, for purposes of determining whether it is appropriate for the subject to regard q as true, it is not relevant whether the subject *appropriately* regards p as true (and appropriately regards it as true that p entails q); what is relevant is merely whether he *regards* p as true. It is the mere regarding of certain propositions as true that can make it appropriate to regard certain other propositions as true.

As I said, this seems to be one legitimate way of thinking about appropriateness. We might say that the standard of local appropriateness focuses on the fact that regarding-as-true is an attitude and that an attitude can be made appropriate by other attitudes.[12] But local appropriateness is not the only legitimate way to think about appropriateness. The idea behind the "global appropriateness" standard is that believing something is a matter of regarding some proposition as *true*, and one cannot appropriately regard a proposition as true unless one has a reason for thinking that it *is* true. According to this view, local appropriateness is not sufficient for appropriateness. Suppose again that a subject believes p and believes p entails q, and thereupon believes q. If the subject does not appropriately believe p, that is, if the subject does not have a reason for thinking that p is true, then even if p does entail q, the subject will not have a reason for thinking that q is true.

So what does it take to have a reason for thinking that a proposition is true? Suppose that the proposition we are concerned with is about the external world, so it is something about the external world that makes the proposition true. If a subject is going to have a reason for thinking that the proposition is true, he must be appropriately connected to the part of the external world that makes the proposition true. I would suggest more specifically that if the subject is going to have a reason for believing that the proposition is true, then his belief must be *intelligibly* connected to some relevant part of the external world. But how *can* his belief be intelligibly connected to a relevant part of the external world? One way to be intelligibly connected to something is to be intelligibly caused by it. States of the external world cannot themselves be intelligible causes, for physical states are not intelligible causes. But states of the external world reveal themselves to us in experiences and rational intuitions, in that relevant intelligible similarity and explanatory relations obtain between experiences and rational intuitions on the one hand and corresponding parts of the external world on the other (sec. 2.4, 2.5, 3.5). So experiences and rational intuitions are intelligibly connected to parts of the external world, even though they are not intelligibly caused by these parts. Moreover, experiences and rational intuitions can be intelligible causes of beliefs (sec. 3.3, 3.5). So insofar as beliefs are intelligibly caused by experiences or rational intuitions, they will be intelligibly connected to the parts of the external world that reveal themselves through these experiences and rational intuitions. I conclude that a subject has a reason for believing a proposition about the external world to be true if and only if the belief is intelligibly caused, either directly or through intermediate beliefs, by an experience or rational intuition. Specifically, a noninferential belief about the external world is held for a reason if and only if it is directly and intelligibly caused by an experience or rational intuition. An inferential belief is held for a reason if and only if it is intelligibly caused, all beliefs in the inferential chain are intelligibly caused, and the beliefs at the end of the chain are intelligibly and directly caused by experiences or rational intuitions. In other words, a subject has a reason for believing a proposition about the external world to be true if and only if the belief is globally appropriate.

As I said, both local appropriateness and global appropriateness are legitimate ways of thinking about appropriateness and rationality, and I don't think there is any sense in which one of these notions is more legitimate than the other. In general we are interested in both of these notions of appropriateness, although in some contexts we might be interested in one notion to the exclusion of the other. So sometimes we might just be interested in the question of whether it is rational for a subject to believe some proposition, *given* the beliefs that he already has. We are interested only in whether it would be rational for the subject to believe *that one proposition*; we are not worried about the rationality of any of his other beliefs. In such a context, we are clearly interested in only local rationality.[13] I think that local rationality may also be the concern of philosophers who advocate a principle of epistemic conservatism.[14] According to those philosophers, a belief can be rational simply in virtue of being held. I am singularly unmoved by this principle; I know of no notion of rationality of interest to us according to which the mere act of believing something can make it rational to do so.

But perhaps those who advocate this principle are really trying to get across the idea that beliefs, whether rational or not, can make *other* beliefs rational simply in virtue of being held. This is just the idea of local appropriateness, according to which the mere regarding of certain propositions as true makes it appropriate to regard certain other propositions as true.

So we do have an interest in local appropriateness and rationality; nevertheless I think it is fair to say that global rationality has special importance for us. As I will explain presently, it is global rationality that is required for knowledge, and knowledge surely does have special importance for us.

4.5   Justification, Rationality, and Intelligible Causation

Some of our beliefs constitute knowledge. Of course, we can only know things that are true; only our true beliefs count as knowledge. But true beliefs are not sufficient for knowledge. I can believe something for all sorts of bad reasons; if such a belief turns out to be true by some lucky accident, that does not make it into knowledge. If my belief is to count as knowledge, I must hold it for good reasons, *appropriate* reasons; my belief must be appropriately held. More familiarly, I need to be *justified* in holding my belief if my belief is to constitute knowledge, and I think it is fair to say that a justified belief is a rational belief.

Justification is one of the requirements for knowledge. The idea that a justified belief is a rational belief is a familiar one; what we need to clarify is the notion of rationality that is being employed here. It is clear that local rationality is not sufficient for justification. Everyone agrees that a "regress problem" arises in connection with justification, but the problem would not arise if justification were local rationality.[15] What is the regress problem? Consider some belief that p; how can it be justified? Presumably one way it can be justified is through rational inference; if there is any knowledge at all, presumably some of it is inferential knowledge. We can say that the belief that p is justified *by* the beliefs from which it is inferred. For purposes of simplicity, let us assume that the belief that p is inferred from just one belief, the belief that q. We now ask: for the belief that p to be justified, is it sufficient that it be rationally inferred from the belief that q? If justification were local rationality, then the answer to this question would be yes, and there would be no regress problem. But in fact almost everyone agrees that this question should be answered in the negative. For the belief that p to be justified, it is not sufficient that it be rationally inferred from the belief that q; in addition, the belief that q must itself be justified. The inference from q to p in effect transfers q's justification to p. So now we face the question of how the belief that q can be justified. If the only way that beliefs can be justified is by inference, then the belief that q will have to be justified by some belief that r from which it is inferred, the belief that r will have to be justified by the belief that s from which it is inferred, and we are well on our way toward a problematic regress of justification. But although the claim that beliefs can be justified only by inference seems to lead to a problematic regress, many have thought that the claim is true. They have held that a justified belief is a rational belief, a rational belief is a belief that is produced by reasoning, and reasoning is just inference. So we seem to have a problem about how beliefs of any kind are justified.

I claim that in fact there is no problem here. Justification is global rationality, and the regress problem can be solved because there can be noninferentially justified beliefs that stop any potentially problematic regresses. Rationality, according to my account, whether local or global, is a matter of appropriateness, and therefore a matter of intelligible causation. As we have seen, inference is not the only way that beliefs can be intelligibly caused; beliefs can also be intelligibly caused by experiences and rational intuitions. If justification is intelligible causation, then beliefs can be noninferentially justified by experiences and rational intuitions in virtue of being intelligibly caused by them. Beliefs can also be inferentially justified by being inferred from beliefs that are noninferentially justified (or by being inferred from beliefs that are themselves inferred from beliefs that are noninferentially justified, etc.). The view that justification is global rationality thus enables us to endorse the traditional foundationalist account of justification. According to this traditional view, there are two kinds of justified beliefs: foundational beliefs that are noninferentially justified, and beliefs that are justified by being inferred from foundational beliefs, either directly or through a chain of inferences. The view that justification is global rationality enables us to endorse foundationalism by showing us why it is the correct account of justification.

The view that justification is global rationality also enables us to respond to standard objections to foundationalism. Perhaps *the* standard objection to foundationalism is that there is something inherently problematic about noninferential justification. The commitment to noninferential justification has been derided as involving a belief in the "myth of the given."[16] But what really is supposed to be wrong with noninferential justification? One thought, which I mentioned earlier, is that justification by its very nature must be inferential, because a justified belief is a rational belief, a rational belief is a belief produced by reasoning, and a belief produced by reasoning is a belief produced by inference. But I have already explained why we must reject the view that rationality is to be understood in terms of reasoning (sec. 4.2).

A different way to formulate what is wrong with noninferential justification goes as follows. If noninferential justification is to put an end to justificatory regresses, then the states that noninferentially justify beliefs must be such as to not themselves require justification. In particular, according to the foundationalist, experiences and rational intuitions can justify beliefs without themselves needing to be justified. The objector claims to find something problematic in the idea of a state that can justify beliefs without itself needing to be justified.[17] But once we understand what justification is all about, we see that there is nothing problematic here. Experiences and rational intuitions can justify beliefs because they can cause them in an intelligible way, and therefore in a way that results in their being appropriately held. Experiences and rational intuitions do not need to be justified themselves because they are not propositional attitudes, and therefore questions of appropriateness do not arise for them.

A different kind of objection to foundationalism is that it leads to skepticism (Greco 1999, 2000). The worry here is that even if experiences can justify beliefs about themselves, they cannot justify beliefs about the external world. But this worry is unfounded: given that intelligible causation is sufficient for justification, experiences can justify beliefs about the external world. As I showed earlier, experiences can intelligibly cause beliefs about the external world (sec. 3.3.3) and can therefore justify such beliefs. Traditional foundationalism can meet the threat of skepticism.

The main rivals to traditional foundationalism are coherentism and reliabilism.[18] The coherentist holds that a belief can be justified only by other beliefs; the belief is justified only if it *coheres* sufficiently with these other beliefs. We have already seen how coherentism results from the mistaken attempt to understand justification and rationality in terms of reasoning (sec. 4.2). The reliabilist holds that a necessary condition for a belief to be justified is that it be reliably (not intelligibly) caused; beliefs are reliably caused when they are produced by a reliable process, a process that *generally* produces true beliefs. The reliabilist does appreciate that some kind of connection holds between justification and truth, but he fails to correctly describe the nature of this connection. Given my view that a justified belief is an appropriately held belief, justification is connected with truth in that a person who holds the justified belief that *p* appropriately regards *p* as true.

Both coherentists and reliabilists fail to take seriously the idea that a justified belief is an appropriately held belief, for they both miss the way in which questions of appropriateness arise for beliefs. Presumably they miss these questions of appropriateness because they fail to consider the intrinsic nature of conscious beliefs and thus fail to see that to hold a belief consciously is to regard a proposition as true, and therefore questions arise as to whether it is appropriate to regard given propositions as true. But once we realize that questions of appropriateness do arise for beliefs, then it is natural to think that a justified belief should be an appropriately held belief. And given that an appropriately held belief is a belief that is intelligibly (not reliably) caused, and given that only experiences, rational intuitions, and beliefs can intelligibly cause beliefs (about the external world), it will be traditional foundationalism that correctly identifies the ways in which beliefs can be justified.[19]

The connection between appropriateness and intelligible causation also explains why justification must be *internalist* in nature. Internalism about justification is the view that only mental states can justify beliefs.[20] The literature discusses inconclusively what the rationale of internalism is supposed to be.[21] On my view, the answer to this question is a straightforward one: only mental states can justify beliefs because only mental states can be intelligible causes of beliefs.

Not only does my account of justification as global rationality and appropriateness explain the sense in which justified beliefs are rational, but it also explains the role of causation in justification. What is the role of causation in justification? Epistemologists sometimes distinguish between two necessary but jointly sufficient conditions for a belief being justified: the believer must *have* justification for the belief, and the belief must be *based* on the justification (Moser 1989, 8). If only the first condition is met, the belief is said to be merely *justifiable*; both conditions must be met if the belief is to be justified (Pollock 1986, 81; Korcz 1997, 171). The justification for a belief is naturally understood as that which makes the belief rational, whereas the basing relation is generally taken to be some kind of causal relation.[22] An adequate theory of justification must provide a unified account of what justification is that explains why both of these conditions must be met for a belief to be justified. Such a unified account has seemed elusive because of the difficulty in discerning how the two conditions could fit together. One condition is concerned with rationality, the other is concerned with causation, and it is not clear how rationality and causation are supposed to be related here.

On my account of justification, it is clear how rationality and causation are related. A justified belief is a rational belief is an appropriately held belief is a belief that is intelligibly caused. A justification for a belief is a state that *can* cause the belief in an intelligible way (and thus make the belief rational); the belief is *based* on the justification if in fact the justification *does* cause the belief in an intelligible way. A justification has the *power* to intelligibly cause a belief, but this causal power, like any causal power, will be exercised only in the presence of certain kinds of initiating conditions,[23] and it is only when the causal power is exercised that the belief is based on the justification. A justification *can* make a belief rational, but it *does* make a belief rational only if it literally *makes*, that is, *causes*, the belief.

Finally, an account of justification should explain why we care about having justified beliefs, for surely we do care about having justified beliefs. Knowledge is surely important to us, and we must understand the importance of knowledge partly in terms of the importance to us of possessing justified beliefs. On my account of justification, we care about justification because justified beliefs are beliefs that are held appropriately, and we care about holding our beliefs appropriately. More generally, it is our nature to take attitudes toward propositions, and we presumably have an interest in holding these attitudes appropriately (sec. 4.2).

But one question remains. Granted that justification is important to us, why should justification be a requirement for *knowledge*? To answer this question, we need to inquire into the nature of knowledge.

4.6   The Unity of Knowledge

Philosophers generally try to understand knowledge in terms of its necessary and jointly sufficient conditions. As we have already seen, if I am to know some proposition p, then it must be the case that (1) I believe p, (2) p is true, and (3) my belief that *p* is justified. Edmund Gettier (1963) is generally thought to have taught us that there is also a fourth condition for knowledge; let us say that for me to know that *p*, it must also be the case that (4) my belief that *p* is Gettierized. Suppose that we should succeed in specifying and explicating these four conditions with sufficient clarity and precision, and suppose also that these four necessary conditions for knowledge were also jointly sufficient. We would still not have an adequate understanding of knowledge, for we would not understand why we possess a concept that includes and unites precisely these four conditions. A belief may possess all sorts of desirable qualities; why, out of all these qualities, did we choose the three qualities of being true, being justified, and being Gettierized and proclaim that beliefs that have these three qualities have a special status: they qualify as knowledge? Presumably it is not just a random accident that we happen to possess a concept that groups together beliefs that possess these three qualities specifically; surely there must be a story to tell of why beliefs that possess these three qualities are of special interest to us. It is this kind of story I was looking for when I asked at the end of the previous section why justification is a requirement for knowledge. Granted that justification is important to us, why should justification get to be part of the concept of knowledge, a concept that unites a privileged few of the qualities that beliefs can possess?

I think that there is a story to be told here; we can give a unified account of the nature of knowledge that explains why knowledge has four necessary but jointly sufficient conditions. Consider Timothy Williamson's suggestive remarks about the connection between belief and knowledge; he states that "belief aspires to knowledge," and "the point of belief is knowledge."[24] Of course, beliefs do not literally aspire to anything, and it is unclear what it means to speak of the "point" of belief. Nevertheless I think that these remarks point us in the right direction. Perhaps the underlying idea here is that beliefs have a certain kind of ideal form, and beliefs qualify as knowledge when they are in this ideal form. What determines the ideal form of beliefs? I suggest that the intrinsic nature of conscious belief is such as to determine certain standards for beliefs. Beliefs that meet these standards count as knowledge. There are three standards for beliefs, and therefore three qualities that beliefs must have to qualify as knowledge (justification, truth, Gettierization); each quality satisfies one of the three standards.

We are already familiar with one of these standards: appropriateness. Recall that conscious beliefs involve acts of consciousness directed toward propositions. The act of consciousness in a belief is instantiated in the form of a determinate kind of attitude toward a proposition, the attitude of regarding the proposition as true. Given the intrinsic nature of this attitude, a question arises as to whether the attitude is being held appropriately (sec. 4.1). In other words, the intrinsic nature of the regarding-as-true attitude is such as to give rise to a standard of appropriateness for beliefs. Beliefs that meet this standard are rational beliefs. In fact, we can distinguish two standards of appropriateness here, and thus we can distinguish two kinds of rationality: local rationality and global rationality (sec. 4.4). Global rationality entails local rationality, but not vice versa. A justified belief is a belief that is globally rational (sec. 4.5). Justified beliefs meet both appropriateness standards for beliefs.[25]

Another standard for beliefs is correctness. Regarding a proposition as true includes representing that proposition to be true. This kind of representation gives rise to a correctness standard: the representation is correct if the proposition is true, and incorrect otherwise. So the regarding-as-true attitude is such as to give rise both to an appropriateness standard and to a correctness standard. A belief meets the correctness standard when it is true, that is, when the believed proposition is true. Beliefs must be both justified and true in order to qualify as knowledge, because beliefs qualify as knowledge when they meet the standards inherent in their status as beliefs, and beliefs must be justified and true in order to meet these standards.

The third standard is also a kind of correctness standard, but applicable specifically to beliefs that meet the first two standards. Thus suppose I believe some proposition p to be true, and I appropriately hold that belief (both locally and globally). I will then have a *reason* for thinking that p is true (sec. 4.4). Moreover, given that my belief is appropriately held, and therefore intelligibly caused, I can also be said to believe p to be true *for* that very reason.

We have just seen that regarding p as true involves representing p to be true. So my reason for regarding p as true is also my reason for representing p to be true; I am representing p to be true for that very reason. We have also just seen that this representation gives rise to a correctness standard for beliefs: if the belief is to be correct, the representation must be correct, and p must be true. But given that I am representing that p is true *for* the reason in question, it follows that the correctness standard in effect extends to the reason, as well: for the belief to be correct, not only must the representation that p is true be correct, but my reason for representing that p is true must also be correct. This is the third standard: the reason that makes the belief appropriate must also be correct.

Insofar as a reason can be correct or incorrect, it must itself be a kind of representation. A reason for thinking a proposition is true is just something that can explain why that proposition is true; it represents: *this* is why the proposition is true. To say that my reason for thinking that p is true is correct is to say that the proposed explanation for why p is true is a correct explanation for why p is true. In general, a belief meets the third standard when the believed proposition is true for the very reason the believer thinks it to be true. Thus an ideal belief must not only meet the appropriateness and correctness standards but also meet what I shall call the *correspondence* standard: the reason the believer has for thinking the proposition is true must correspond to a reason that (truly) explains why the believed proposition is true. We can say that the correspondence standard ensures that the belief's correctness and the belief's appropriateness correspond in the appropriate manner: the reason that makes the belief *appropriate* must explain why the belief is *correct* (true). (What this comes down to in practice is that the beliefs that contribute to the justification of a belief must be true beliefs, and the experiences and rational intuitions that contribute to the justification of a belief must be veridical.)

Knowledge is ideal belief; it is belief that meets the three standards inherent in the nature of belief. Knowledge is true, justified, Gettierized belief because true, justified, Gettierized beliefs meet these three standards. Specifically, true beliefs meet the correctness standard, justified beliefs meet the appropriateness standard, and Gettierized beliefs meet the correspondence standard. Strictly speaking, Gettierized beliefs are beliefs that are not vulnerable to Gettier counterexamples. Gettier counterexamples are just cases of true, justified beliefs that do not qualify as knowledge. But I submit that what is characteristic of Gettier counterexamples is that they fail to meet the correspondence standard: the reason that justifies the belief fails to explain why

the belief is true.[26] Only beliefs that meet the correspondence
standard will be invulnerable to such counterexamples. So Gettierized beliefs do meet the correspondence standard.

Consciousness is important to us because it enables us to know
the world. On the one hand, consciousness enables knowledge
in that rationality is required for knowledge, and only conscious
states can make our beliefs rational (sec. 4.1). But consciousness
makes knowledge possible in an even more fundamental way,
for knowledge just is the ideal form of conscious belief. Knowledge is so important to us because it is important to us that we
be able to hold our conscious beliefs in ideal form. Of course, it
is important to us that we are able to hold beliefs in any form:
we value our ability to interact with the world by consciously
regarding propositions as being true. But we especially value our
ability to hold these attitudes in correct and appropriate ways.

5 The Importance of Consciousness II: Desire, Feeling, and Value

5.1 Desire, Rational Desire, and Value

Consciousness is important to us because of its intelligibility, and we are now beginning to understand why the intelligibility of consciousness is so important to us. Consciousness enables us to take up attitudes toward propositions (sec. 3.4), and at least for some of these attitudes, questions arise as to whether these attitudes are appropriately held. It is here that the intelligibility of consciousness becomes relevant, for as we saw in the previous chapter, our attitudes will be appropriate and rational insofar as they are intelligibly caused by conscious states (sec. 4.1). Intelligible causation becomes important to us once we realize that intelligible causation is what renders our attitudes appropriate and rational.

The foregoing suggests that if we are to attain a complete understanding of how consciousness contributes to the richness of our lives, we need to understand all the various kinds of attitudes that we can take toward propositions, and the corresponding standards of appropriateness that apply to them. I will not attempt such a comprehensive survey here but will instead focus on two of the more central kinds of propositional attitudes. I discussed belief in the previous chapter, and in this chapter I focus on desire, which we can view as a kind of complementary state to belief. If in belief we regard propositions as true, when we desire, we regard propositions as *to be made true*.[1]

We are all familiar with the phenomenon of desire. To desire something, in the relevant sense, is just to want it to happen. I have all sorts of desires: I want to have hamburgers for dinner, I want to learn to play the guitar when I retire, I want to visit my sister later in the year, I want various politicians to win various elections. I am not restricted to regarding certain propositions as being true; regardless of whether they are true, I can want them to be true, I can desire that they become true, or, in other words, I can regard them as to be made true.

Are there standards of appropriateness for desires? This question is somewhat more difficult to answer than the corresponding question about beliefs. As we have seen, it is clear that a question can arise as to whether some typical belief that *p* is appropriate. When I believe that *p*, I regard *p* as being true, but whether *p* is in fact true is typically not up to me (it is a fact about the world, not about myself), so the question can arise as to whether it is appropriate for me to regard *p* as true (sec. 4.1). But it is not clear that any comparable considerations could make it inappropriate for me to regard *p* as to be made true. Whether *p* is to be made true does not seem to be a matter of some fact obtaining about the world (it does not seem to be a matter of any fact obtaining at all), and so the issue of whether *p* is to be made true does not typically seem to be "not up to me" in a way that might give rise to the question of whether it is appropriate for me to regard *p* as to be made true.

Of course, atypical cases will arise in which whether *p* is to be made true is out of my control, and in such cases the question can arise as to whether it is appropriate for me to regard p as to be made true. For example, some propositions are impossible: they *cannot be* true, and therefore they cannot be *made* true. If I have reason to think that a proposition is impossible, then presumably it would be inappropriate for me to regard it as to be made true. I want it to be the case that the square root of two is a rational number, but this desire is inappropriate and irrational. Moreover, some propositions cannot be made true even though they are not impossible. The past might have been different, but it cannot be changed. So although it might have been the case that Abraham Lincoln was not murdered, that Abraham Lincoln was not murdered cannot be made true. Therefore it would be inappropriate and irrational for me to regard this proposition as to be made true. In general, propositions that cannot be made true can be characterized as *unattainable* propositions. And we can say that questions of appropriateness do arise for desires for the unattainable: if I have reason to think that a proposition is unattainable (cannot be made true), then it would be inappropriate for me to regard that proposition as to be made true.[2] (By contrast, there is nothing inappropriate about wishing for the unattainable; desires and wishes are different kinds of propositional attitudes [Velleman 1992, 17] and therefore have different standards of appropriateness.)

But the more interesting question is whether questions of appropriateness can arise with respect to desires for the attainable. If I desire for something to happen that can happen, or if I want to do something that can be done, can any further question of appropriateness then arise with respect to my desire? Equivalently, given that questions of appropriateness with respect to propositional attitudes just are questions of rationality (sec. 4.1), are desires subject to rational criticism? Hume is famous for answering this question in the negative;[3] in the language I am using, he insisted that questions of appropriateness cannot arise for desires. But questions of appropriateness certainly seem to arise for desires. Typically, when someone wants something, it can be appropriate to ask the person why she wants it. For example, if my friend's daughter wants to be a doctor, I can ask her why she wants to be a doctor. If my colleague wants a certain politician to win a certain election, I can ask her why she wants that politician to win. These questions just are questions about the appropriateness of the desires. They are not mere requests for the etiology of the desires but requests to explain how the desires in question can be seen as intelligible, reasonable, and rational.[4]

Given that such questions *do* arise, we still want to understand *how* such questions can arise. Earlier my comparison of belief and desire suggested that there is a difficulty in understanding how such questions can arise. To believe p is to regard p as true, and since it is not up to me whether p is true, a question can arise as to whether it is appropriate for me to regard p as true; whereas to desire that p is to regard p as to be made true, and it is not clear why any question should arise as to whether it is appropriate for me to regard p as to be made true. Nevertheless, I claim, a question can arise as to whether it is appropriate for me to regard p as to be made true. A question can arise as to whether it is appropriate for the *proposition p* to be made true, and therefore a corresponding question can arise as to whether it is appropriate for *me to regard p* as to be made true. Regardless of whether p *is* to be made true, it may be *inappropriate* for p to be made true, and if so, it may also be inappropriate for me to regard p as to be made true. Note the different ways in which questions of appropriateness arise for beliefs and desires. In the case of belief, the question of appropriateness arises directly for the attitude: given that it is not up to me whether p is true, it may be inappropriate for me to regard p as true. But in the case of desire, the question of appropriateness arises first for the proposition, and then, as a consequence, for the attitude toward that proposition. When I regard p as to be made true, the question that arises is whether it is appropriate for p to be made true. If I can answer this question in the affirmative, then not only will it be appropriate for p to be made true, but it will also be appropriate for me to regard p as to be made true. If I answer this question in the negative, however, it will be inappropriate both for p to be made true and for me to regard p as to be made true. Questions do arise as to the appropriateness of desires, but these questions arise only because corresponding questions arise as to the appropriateness of the objects of desire, and it is the answers to these latter questions that determine the answers to the former questions.

What determines the answers to the latter questions; what makes objects of desire appropriate or inappropriate? Their value, of course. It is appropriate that propositions be made true if they are desirable, worthwhile, in short, good.[5] It is inappropriate that propositions be made true if they are undesirable, worthless, or bad. (On the contrary, it is appropriate that bad things be prevented or eliminated.) If I then have *reason* to think that some proposition is good, then it will be appropriate and rational for me to regard that proposition as to be made true. And if I have reason to think that some proposition is bad, then it will be inappropriate and irrational for me to regard that proposition as to be made true. In short, it is rational to desire the good, and irrational to desire the bad.

I am not claiming that to desire something is to *regard* it as being good.[6] To desire something is to regard it as to be made true. Although goodness and badness enter into the standard of appropriateness for desires, they do not enter into the characterization of desire itself. Nevertheless goodness and badness enter into the standard of appropriateness for desires *in virtue* of the nature of desire itself, for it is the intrinsic nature of propositional attitudes that determines the standards that apply to those attitudes (sec. 4.5). The intrinsic nature of desiring a proposition is a matter of regarding that proposition as to be made true, but since the nature of goodness (positive value) is such as to make it appropriate that good propositions be made true, and since the nature of badness (negative value) is such as to make it inappropriate for bad propositions to be made true, it follows that the nature of desire is such as to make value relevant to their standard of appropriateness. Therefore it is because of our capacity to desire that we care so much about value, for it is important to many of us that our desires be appropriate; and for our desires to be appropriate, we need to have reason to think that the objects of our desires have positive value.

We therefore need to understand how we can have reason to think that the objects of our desires have value. A desire is appropriate and rational when we have reason to think that it is a desire for something of value, just as a belief is appropriate and rational when we have reason to think that it is a belief in something that is true. But what is the nature of such reasons; what are the conditions under which they obtain? We learned in the previous chapter how to answer such questions. We understand the nature of rational belief by understanding rationality in terms of appropriateness, and appropriateness in terms of intelligible causation; we then investigate the conditions under which beliefs can be intelligibly caused. Similarly, if we are to understand the nature of rational desire, if we are to understand how we can have reasons for thinking that the objects of our desires have value, we need to investigate the conditions under which our desires can be intelligibly caused. Let us proceed to do so.

5.2   Two Kinds of Rational Desires

So far all our examples of intelligible causation have involved the production of belief. Do we have any reason to think that desires can be intelligibly caused, as well? Which of our desires are intelligibly caused, and how does such intelligible causation take place? Here we might look to our examples of intelligible production of belief for guidance, for perhaps desires can be intelligibly caused in ways analogous to those in which beliefs are intelligibly caused.

Many philosophers believe that there are processes of "practical" inference or reasoning that are similar to the processes of (theoretical) inference that produce beliefs. Given that some processes of theoretical inference can intelligibly produce beliefs (sec. 3.4), perhaps there are processes of practical inference that can intelligibly produce desires. Consider an example of a kind of desire that many would acknowledge to be appropriate and rational in some sense: an instrumental desire, that is, a person's desire for a means to achieve one of his ends (i.e., a means to satisfy one of his other desires). Suppose I desire to go to medical school because I want to be a doctor, and I believe that going to medical school is a requirement for being a doctor. I suggest that given that I want to be a doctor and given that I believe that going to medical school is a requirement for being a doctor, then it is rational for me to want to go to medical school. That I want to be a doctor and believe that going to medical school is a requirement for being a doctor makes it rational for me to want to go to medical school. But how does this fact make it rational for me to have this desire? It is in this context that some have introduced the notion of a practical inference. Just as a valid theoretical inference can make rational the belief that is the result of such inference, so too it is thought that a valid practical inference can make rational the desire (or intention, or action) that results from such practical inference. The problem here is that it is notoriously difficult to make sense of this idea of a valid practical inference. It is characteristic of an inference that the propositional content of the conclusion of the infer- ence stands in appropriate logical relations to the propositional contents of the premises of the inference, logical relations that enable the propositional content of the conclusion to be validly inferred from the propositional contents of the premises. But it is not clear how to construe the propositional contents of desires in such a way as to enable the propositional content of an instru- mental desire to be validly inferred from the propositional con- tents of an appropriate belief–desire pair.[7]

I do not concern myself with this problem here, for I believe that if we are to understand how an instrumental desire is made rational by an appropriate belief–desire pair, we need to take a different approach. I have already argued that in the case of theoretical inference, a belief that is validly inferred from other beliefs is made rational by those beliefs insofar as it is intelligi- bly caused by those beliefs (sec. 4.2). Similarly, I claim that an instrumental desire is made rational by a belief–desire pair inso- far as that pair intelligibly causes the instrumental desire. Desires *can* be intelligibly caused; in particular, instrumental desires can be intelligibly caused by certain belief–desire pairs. In the case of theoretical inference, the idea was that someone who believes both p and (p entails q) would have the intelligible causal power to come to believe q, for the intrinsic nature of the relevant beliefs is such that it is intelligible that someone who simultaneously consciously regards p as true and consciously regards it as true that if p is true, then q must be true, can then come to regard q as being true, as well. Similarly, I am claiming that if a subject simultaneously has the conscious desire that p and the conscious belief that q is a requirement for p, then the intrinsic nature of the desire and belief are such that the subject has the intelligible causal power to come to desire that q. Given that the subject consciously regards p as to be made true, and simultaneously consciously regards it as true that q is a requirement for p, then it is intelligible that the subject can come to regard q as to be made true. I am not claiming that the subject definitely *will* come to regard q as to be made true; the subject has the intelligible causal power to form the desire that q, but conditions might be such as to prevent this power from being exercised (perhaps the subject has a desire for r that conflicts with her desire for p). What I am claiming is that the subject *can* come to regard q as to be made true, and that it would be intelligible for the subject to come to do so; in other words, the subject has the intelligible causal power to do so. There is no need for us to say that the subject who comes to desire q has *inferred* the content of this instrumental desire from the contents of the desire and belief that produced it. What counts is not whether the process that produced this desire is an inferential process but that it is an intelligible process, and therefore a process that makes the desire produced by this process one that is rational and appropriately held.

Instrumental desires are not the only kinds of desires that can be intelligibly caused. Regardless of whether there is such a thing as practical inference, surely there is such a thing as practical *reasoning*, or, if one prefers, practical *deliberation*. We do deliberate about the practical, that is, about what to do. The conclusion of such deliberation can be a belief that some particular course of action is the best thing to do (an evaluative belief). Such a belief makes it rational to desire to perform that course of action.[8] I claim that the way an evaluative belief makes it rational and appropriate to have this corresponding desire is through its ability to *intelligibly produce* such a desire, for as we have seen, it is appropriate that a proposition be made true if it would be a good thing for it to be made true (sec. 5.1). So if I believe, that is, regard it as true, that my performing some course of action is not only good but best, then surely it will be appropriate for me to regard it as to be made true that I perform such action. The belief can make the desire appropriate insofar as the belief can intelligibly cause the desire.

So we now have two ways in which desires can be intelligibly caused and thereby be rational. An instrumental desire can be intelligibly caused by an appropriate belief–desire pair, and a desire to do something can be intelligibly caused by an evaluative belief that such action is the best thing to do. Nevertheless, although these intelligibly caused desires seem to be rational, their rationality can also be questioned. Consider first the desire that is based on an evaluative belief. One might point out that if it is to be rational for me to regard some p as to be made true, it is not sufficient for me to regard it as true that p is good; I need to have a *reason* to think that p is good (sec. 5.1). And if the evaluative belief is not itself rational, then I will not have such a reason. (Perhaps an evaluative belief produced by practical deliberation will be rational, but it is not clear that it has to be.) A similar objection can be made with regard to the purported rationality of the intelligibly caused instrumental desire. Again, suppose I am intelligibly caused to desire that q by my desire for p and my belief that q is a requirement for p. One might object that if my desire that q is to be rational, I need to have a reason for thinking that q is good, but I will have a reason for thinking that q is good only if I already have a reason for thinking that p is good. But if my desire for p is not itself rational, then I will not have a reason for thinking that p is good. The idea behind both of these objections is the same: for a desire to be rational, it is not sufficient that it be intelligibly caused; it needs to be intelligibly caused by *rational* beliefs and desires.

Recall that in chapter 4 we considered a similar objection to the idea that certain inferential beliefs were rational (sec. 4.4). The concern there was that an inferential belief intelligibly caused would not be rational unless the beliefs from which it was inferred were themselves rational. My response to this concern was that we possess two different notions of rationality for beliefs, local and global rationality, and that a belief can be locally rational and globally irrational. A belief is locally rational if it is intelligibly caused, whereas a belief is globally rational if, in addition to being intelligibly caused, all its causes, both direct and remote, for which a question of rationality arises are themselves intelligibly caused. We can now see that this distinction between local and global rationality applies to desires as well as to beliefs. Just as an inferential belief is globally rational if it is intelligibly caused, and if all the beliefs in the causal chain of inference are themselves intelligibly caused, so too a desire is globally rational if it is intelligibly caused, and if all the beliefs and desires that are among its direct or remote causes are themselves intelligibly caused.

We can now employ this distinction to explain the conflicting intuitions we may have about the rationality of certain kinds of desires. Consider, for example, the desire that is intelligibly caused by an unjustified evaluative belief. We have conflicting intuitions here because the desire is rational according to one notion of rationality, but irrational according to a different notion of rationality. Specifically, the desire is locally rational but globally irrational.

The distinction between local and global rationality can also help us to illuminate the debate among philosophers about whether "we have reason to do what will satisfy our desires" (Schueler 1995, 110). Some philosophers hold that desires provide reasons for action, whereas others claim that desires do not provide reasons for action.[9] Now, we have been concerned here with the rationality of desire, not with the rationality of action. But I think that our discussion of the rationality of desire puts us in a position to diagnose this related debate about the rationality of action. The question about whether desires provide reasons for action parallels the question we have been considering about whether an instrumental desire is made rational by an appropriate belief–desire pair. In discussing this question, we noted considerations both for and against the claim that an instrumental desire is made rational in this manner. I now suggest that the way to resolve these opposing considerations is to acknowledge that two notions of rationality are at play here. An instrumental desire is made locally rational by an appropriate belief–desire pair, but the instrumental desire can be globally rational only if the rationalizing belief and desire are themselves rational. Similarly, I am also suggesting that those who claim that desires can provide reasons *for action* are concerned with local rationality, whereas those who claim the opposite are concerned with global rationality. Desires *do* provide reasons for action in the sense that an action to satisfy some desire can be made locally rational by the desire if the action is intelligibly caused by that desire.[10] Desires *do not* provide reasons for action in the sense that desires are themselves states for which questions of rationality arise, and therefore desires cannot make actions globally rational unless they themselves are globally rational. Moreover, it must be something other than some further desire that makes a desire globally rational, for only something for which a question of rationality does not arise can end the "chain of rationality" in the way required for global rationality. Therefore it will also be something other than a desire that makes an action globally rational. Both those who claim that desires provide reasons for action and those who claim that desires do not provide reasons for action are correct, but they are correct with respect to different notions of rationality. There is no substantive debate here.

But there is a substantive debate in the vicinity. Some philosophers who claim that desires provide reasons for action go further and claim that *only* desires can provide reasons for action; I refer to this claim as *internalism*.[11] Given my way of formulating these issues, we can understand the internalist as claiming that it is impossible for actions (or desires) to be globally rational. For an action to be globally rational, the desire that rationalizes it must itself be globally rational, and as we just saw, only something other than a desire could make the desire globally rational. But in saying that only desires can be reasons for actions, the internalist is in effect saying that there is nothing that can make a desire globally rational, and therefore there is nothing that can make an action globally rational. The internalist would allow that a desire can be made locally rational by an evaluative belief, but then he would hold that this evaluative belief can itself be made rational only by further desires (or perhaps by desires and beliefs). Ultimately, according to the internalist, the rationality of actions must be derived from noninstrumental desires that cannot be made rational by further desires (because they are noninstrumental), and cannot be made rational by anything else (because nothing other than a desire can be a reason for action).

Those who oppose internalists are known as *externalists*; they hold that things other than desires (and evaluative beliefs) can be reasons for action.[12] These other things can not only make actions rational but make them globally rational, and they can make desires globally rational. So there is a substantive debate between internalists and externalists about reasons for action.

What is the attraction of internalism; why would someone hold that nothing other than a belief–desire pair or an evaluative belief can make a desire rational? Recall that in my view a desire is rationally held only insofar as it is intelligibly caused. What underlies the internalist view, I suggest, is the intuition that the only things that can intelligibly cause desires are belief–desire pairs and evaluative beliefs (and the only things that can intelligibly cause evaluative beliefs are desires and beliefs). Such an intuition might initially appear plausible. Perhaps I have succeeded in convincing you that desires can be intelligibly caused by belief–desire pairs and evaluative beliefs, but it is not clear that there are any other candidates for mental states that can intelligibly cause desires. Nor is it clear that we will find any additional candidates if we look to the mental states that can intelligibly cause beliefs, for although experiences and rational intuitions can intelligibly cause beliefs (sec. 3.3, 3.5), it is not at all obvious that they can intelligibly cause desires.[13]

Nevertheless, despite the initial plausibility of internalism, we should not rush to embrace it. As we have already begun to see, internalism has some unattractive consequences. In particular, a consequence of internalism is that all our desires are globally irrational. Surely we should not welcome this consequence. Given that we hold attitudes toward propositions, we presumably care about holding these attitudes appropriately, but if internalism is correct, then there is a sense in which we never hold our desire attitudes appropriately: we never appropriately regard propositions as to be made true. Recall that it will be appropriate and rational for me to regard a proposition as to be made true only if I have a reason for thinking that it would be a good thing for the proposition to be made true (sec. 5.1). And if all our desires are globally irrational, then the reasons I can have here will at best be limited and partial. At best, if my desire for p is locally rational, I can have a reason for thinking that it would be a good thing for p to be made true in the sense that I can have other attitudes (desires and beliefs) that make it appropriate for me to regard p as to be made true. But given that my desire for p is globally irrational, it follows that some of these other attitudes will be inappropriately held (or will be caused by attitudes that are inappropriately held, or will be caused by attitudes that are caused by attitudes that are inappropriately held, etc.). So my reason for thinking that p is a good thing is a reason only relative to other attitudes I have, and some of these other attitudes will not themselves be supported by reasons. But surely we would prefer that our reasons not be merely *relative* in this way.

Recall what is required for having a nonrelative reason for thinking that some proposition *is* true; in other words, recall the requirements for globally rational *beliefs*. If I am to have a non-relative reason for thinking that a proposition about the external world is true, then I need to stand in an intelligible connection to a relevant part of the external world (sec. 4.4). Similarly, I

suggest that if I am to have a globally rational desire for something, I need to have a reason for thinking that the object of my
desire has value in the sense that I need to be standing in an
intelligible connection to the object of my desire and its value,
and not merely to other attitudes I hold. It is not clear whether
such intelligible connections are possible. But I think that we
should put some effort into looking for intelligible connections
of this kind before we despair of finding any. It is to this task
that I now turn. In the remainder of this chapter, I mean to show
that internalism is incorrect: there are things other than beliefs
and desires that can intelligibly cause desires, and these other
things can make our desires globally rational and can give us
nonrelative reasons for thinking that the objects of our desires
have value.

5.3   Bodily Sensations: Pleasures and Pains

The task of finding states other than beliefs and desires that
can intelligibly cause desires can be separated into two distinct
inquiries. Recall that a desire is appropriately and rationally held
if it is intelligibly caused. But we have seen that we can also
think of rational desire as follows: a desire of mine is rational
if I have a reason for thinking that the object of my desire is
good. And in the previous section I suggested that if the reason
in question is to make my desire *globally* rational, then I need to
stand in an intelligible connection to the object of desire itself.
So the inquiry into whether there are states other than beliefs
and desires that can intelligibly cause desires is at the same
time an inquiry into how we can be intelligibly connected to
the objects of our desires. Now, I submit that how we address
the latter inquiry will depend on whether the object of desire

is something mental or something physical (i.e., nonmental), for only mental states can be intelligible causes, and so, a fortiori, only mental states can be intelligible causes of desires. So to understand how we can be intelligibly connected to the *physical* objects of our desires, what we need to understand is how our desires being intelligibly caused by certain mental states can at the same time intelligibly connect us to something physical. I leave this question for the next section.

In this section, I concern myself with understanding how we can be intelligibly connected to the mental objects of our desires. In other words, I wish to understand how a desire of mine, in virtue of being intelligibly caused by something other than a belief or desire, can also be intelligibly connected to the mental item that enters into the propositional content of the desire. The hope here is that there will be a relatively straightforward connection between the mental item that intelligibly causes my desire and the mental item *that* I desire. So perhaps there is a kind of mental state such that when I have a mental state of that kind, I am intelligibly caused to desire that it continue. The idea would then be that in virtue of being intelligibly caused by that mental state to have such a desire, I am intelligibly connected to that mental state and its goodness in a way that gives me a reason to think that it would be a good thing for that mental state to continue. Similarly, perhaps there are mental states of a different kind such that when I have a mental state of that kind, I am intelligibly caused to desire that it cease. The corresponding idea here would be that in virtue of being intelligibly caused by that mental state to desire that it cease, I am intelligibly connected to that mental state and its badness in a way that gives me a reason to think that it would be a good thing for that mental state to cease.

Do we have any reason to think that there are mental states of these kinds? What we need to look for are mental states that both cause desires and enter into the propositional contents of those desires. Once we find mental states of these kinds, perhaps we will find support for the idea that these mental states are also *intelligible* causes of the desires that they cause.

In fact, we are familiar with mental states of these kinds: our pleasurable and painful bodily sensations. When I experience a painful sensation, I typically want it to stop, whereas pleasurable sensations often produce in me desires for them to continue. For example, my wife caresses me in a certain way on the nape of my neck, and I wish the sensation would last forever. By contrast, I accidentally cut my finger, and I desperately want the pain to stop. But not only do bodily pains and pleasures produce desires that refer in these ways to the sensations that cause them, but we also take these desires to be reasonable ones. In my terminology, we take them to be appropriate and rational.[14] As I noted earlier (sec. 5.1), typically when a person wants something, it is appropriate to ask the person why she wants it. If Jerry wants to be a doctor, I can ask him why he wants to be a doctor. But it would be inappropriate, and even strange and off-putting, to be asked why we want our bodily pains to cease and why we want our pleasurable sensations to continue. We take it to be obvious to everyone that such desires are appropriate; it just *makes sense* to want a pain to stop and a pleasurable sensation to continue. And we take it to be obvious *why* our desires for our pains to cease and for our pleasurable sensations to continue are appropriate—because of the ways that these sensations feel. Given the way pain feels, it makes sense to want it to stop; given the way pleasurable sensations feel, it makes sense to want them to continue.

I submit that it is no coincidence that our painful and pleasurable sensations both cause desires about themselves and make such desires appropriate. I claim that it is in virtue of the *way* these sensations cause such desires that they make the desires appropriate; specifically, they cause these desires in an intelligible way. A desire that a certain pain stop is appropriate insofar as it is an appropriate and intelligible response to that pain, and it is an intelligible response *to* that pain insofar as the pain intelligibly causes the desire.[15]

Recall that our goal in this section is to understand how desires can be globally rational. Specifically, we wish to understand how I can have a reason for thinking the object of my desire is good in virtue of being intelligibly connected to the object of my desire and its value. We are now in a position to understand how such a thing is possible. Suppose that my desire that a pleasurable sensation continue is intelligibly caused by that very sensation. Since sensations are not themselves propositional attitudes for which questions of appropriateness arise, the desire will be not only rational but globally rational. Insofar as my desire is rational, I will have a reason for thinking that the object of my desire is good; that is, I will have a reason for thinking that it is a good thing for that pleasurable sensation to continue. Insofar as my desire is *globally* rational, I have this reason in virtue of standing in an intelligible connection to that pleasurable sensation and its goodness. I stand in an intelligible connection to the pleasurable sensation insofar as my desire is intelligibly caused by that pleasurable sensation. And, I claim, I stand in an intelligible connection to the *goodness* of the pleasurable sensation in that the property of the sensation that makes it good is the intrinsic categorical property of the sensation that intelligibly grounds its power to cause the desire. This categorical property of the sensation is the way the sensation feels. Similarly, when I have a desire that some painful sensation cease, and the desire is intelligibly caused by the pain, then I have a reason for thinking that it would be a good thing for the pain to cease in virtue of standing in an intelligible connection to the pain and its badness. And I stand in this intelligible connection insofar as my desire is intelligibly caused by the pain, and insofar as the property of the pain that makes it bad is the intrinsic categorical property of the pain that intelligibly grounds its power to cause the desire: the way the pain feels.[16]

These ideas need to be elaborated. First, let me say something about the nature of these categorical properties of painful and pleasurable sensations that intelligibly ground their powers to produce corresponding desires. Bodily sensations are similar in their nature to perceptual experiences. Whereas a (nonhallucinatory) perceptual experience consists in a subject being conscious of observable properties being instantiated in a physical object (sec. 2.3), a (nonhallucinatory) bodily sensation consists in a subject being conscious of what we might call *sensational* properties being instantiated in some part of the subject's body. So when I have a pain in my toe, I am conscious of a painful feeling, or, equivalently, a painful sensation, in my toe. This painful feeling is what I am referring to as a sensational property, and this feeling is *in* my toe in the sense that it is a property of my toe. Terms such as "sensation" and "feeling" can apply both to the sensational properties of my body of which I am conscious and to the mental states that consist in my being conscious of such properties. There are different kinds of painful sensational properties (and different kinds of pleasurable sensational properties) just as there are, say, a variety of different sensory colors. Being a painful feeling is a determinable property; just as the different colors are all similar to each other in a certain way in virtue of all being colors, so too the different painful feelings are all similar to each other in a certain way in virtue of all being painful feelings.[17]

Bodily sensations, like all conscious states, have phenomenal character. And just as a perceptual experience has phenomenal properties that are intelligibly determined by its observable properties, so too there are phenomenal properties of bodily sensations that are intelligibly determined by their sensational properties. So when I have a painful feeling in my toe, the phenomenal property consisting of what it is like for me to be conscious of the painful feeling in my toe will be intelligibly determined by the nature of that painful feeling in my toe. I will refer to this kind of phenomenal property as a *phenomenal pain* property. And similarly there are *phenomenal pleasure* properties that are intelligibly determined by the pleasurable sensations we feel in our body parts. As we would expect, there are different kinds of phenomenal pain and pleasure properties corresponding to the different kinds of painful and pleasurable sensational properties.

Now, just as the phenomenal properties of perceptual experiences intelligibly ground their causal powers to produce certain kinds of beliefs (sec. 3.3), so too the phenomenal properties of painful and pleasurable bodily sensations intelligibly ground their causal powers to produce certain kinds of desires. Specifically, the phenomenal pain property of a painful sensation intelligibly grounds its power to produce a desire for the sensation to cease, and the phenomenal pleasure property of a pleasurable sensation intelligibly grounds its power to produce a desire for that sensation to continue. Earlier I stated that it was the way a painful or pleasurable sensation *feels* that intelligibly grounds its causal power to produce an appropriate desire. My talk of the way a sensation feels should be understood as referring to the phenomenal character of the sensation, for it is the way the pain feels *to me*, that is, what it is like for me to be conscious of the pain, that makes it intelligible for me to want the pain to stop. And similarly, given the way a pleasurable sensation feels, it is intelligible that I would want the pleasurable sensation to continue.

Let me be clear as to what I am claiming about painful and pleasurable sensations, and what I am not claiming. I am claiming that they have the intelligible power to produce certain kinds of desires; I am not claiming that these powers are always exercised. (And I am certainly not claiming that when these powers are exercised and the desires are produced, the desires are always acted on.) Suppose I am experiencing pain while undergoing a medical procedure. The pain is genuinely unpleasant, though tolerable. I want the medical procedure to continue, and I therefore want the pain to continue because I realize that the pain is a necessary consequence of the procedure. Now, perhaps I am conflicted here, and I also have a desire for the pain to stop. But I need not be conflicted; I may have no desire for the pain to stop. If I do not, this circumstance is no counterexample to my claim, for I am claiming only that pains have the causal power to produce desires for the pain to stop; I am not claiming that this causal power is always exercised.[18]

Of course, those who are willing to acknowledge that painful and pleasurable sensations have these causal powers may yet resist the idea that these causal powers are intelligible. But remember why we found it plausible to suggest that these causal powers are intelligible. Not only do these bodily sensations cause these desires, but we regard the desires in question as reasonable and appropriate desires. We need the idea of intelligible causation to make sense of the idea of appropriate desires (sec. 4.1, 5.1). Specifically, the desires are appropriate *responses to* the sensations. A desire is a response to a sensation insofar as it is caused by that sensation. What I am suggesting is that a response can be appropriate only if the causation is intelligible. The thesis that painful and pleasurable sensations can intelligibly cause desires best makes sense of the familiar facts that these sensations do cause desires, and the desires in question are appropriate ones.

Thus painful and pleasurable sensations can intelligibly cause desires, and the desires intelligibly caused by these sensations are globally rational. As I noted earlier, a desire that is globally rational stands in an intelligible connection to the object of the desire and its value. Now that we have a better understanding of how certain kinds of sensations intelligibly cause desires that pertain to those very sensations, we can also better understand how these desires can stand in intelligible connections to those sensations and their value. Consider my desire that the pleasurable sensation in the nape of my neck last forever, a desire that is intelligibly caused by that very sensation. My desire is rational, and I thereby have a reason for thinking that it would be a good thing for that pleasurable sensation to continue. We can say that it would be a good thing for that pleasurable sensation to continue insofar as the pleasurable sensation is itself a good thing. So insofar as my desire is globally rational, I, through my desire, need to be intelligibly connected to that sensation and its goodness. Since my desire is intelligibly caused by the sensation, it will be intelligibly connected to it. But in what sense am I intelligibly connected to the goodness of the sensation, that is, to the property of the sensation that makes it good (i.e., the property of the sensation on which its goodness supervenes)? Consider the following: in addition to being intelligibly connected to the sensation as a whole, I am intelligibly connected to a certain property of the sensation, the categorical property that intelligibly grounds the sensation's power to cause my desire. This property is the phenomenal pleasure property of the sensation, the way the sensation feels to me. Now, if this property is the property that makes the sensation good, then in being intelligibly connected to this property, I am intelligibly connected to the goodness of the sensation.

Given everything else we have said, however, it *is* plausible to think that it is the way a pleasurable sensation feels to its possessor (what it is like for the possessor to feel the sensation) that makes it good. It is plausible to think that the categorical property of a pleasurable sensation that intelligibly grounds its power to produce a desire that the sensation continue is also the property that gives the sensation its positive value. Consider: in virtue of being intelligibly caused by the sensation to want it to continue, I have a reason for thinking that the sensation is good. And perhaps the idea here is that I have this reason when I form the desire insofar as my formation of this desire is a *response* to the goodness of the sensation; it is a manifestation of my *sensitivity* to the value of the sensation. But I cannot respond to the goodness of the sensation unless the goodness of the sensation, the property that makes it good, causes me to have this response. So the property that causes me to have this response will also be the property that makes the sensation good. Now, the property of the sensation that causes this response is the way the sensation feels, so the way the sensation feels will also be the property that makes the sensation good.

In further support of this idea, recall that I have already noted the naturalness of saying that it is the way a pleasurable sensation feels that makes it appropriate to want the sensation to continue. But if it is appropriate for me to want a sensation to continue, then I have a reason to think that the sensation is good. And so if it is the way the sensation feels that makes it appropriate for me to want it to continue, then presumably it is also the way the sensation feels that constitutes its goodness.

Parallel remarks apply to desires for painful sensations to cease that are intelligibly caused by those sensations. The only difference here is that whereas I have a reason for thinking that it would be a good thing for the pleasurable sensation to continue in virtue of being intelligibly connected to the sensation and its goodness, here I will have a reason to think that it would be a good thing for some painful sensation to cease in virtue of being intelligibly connected to the pain and its badness. What makes it a good thing for a pain to cease is the fact that the pain is bad. And when I have a desire for a painful sensation to cease that is intelligibly caused by that sensation, I will be intelligibly connected to what makes the pain bad insofar as I am intelligibly connected to the categorical property of the pain that intelligibly grounds its power to produce the desire, for it is this categorical property of the pain that makes it bad. This categorical property is the phenomenal pain property of the sensation, the way that the pain feels to me. What makes a painful sensation bad is the way it feels to its possessor, just as what makes a pleasurable sensation good is the way it feels to its possessor.[19]

I have now succeeded in explaining how there can be globally rational desires. There *are* states other than beliefs and desires that can intelligibly cause desires. In particular, I have explained how desires that concern mental items can be globally rational. Our desires for our pleasurable sensations to continue and for our painful sensations to cease can be globally rational insofar as we are able to be intelligibly connected to these sensations and their value. We are sensitive to the value of our painful and pleasurable sensations. The more difficult question is whether we can be sensitive to the value of physical things out there in the external world.

5.4 Feelings

My aim in this section is to explain how noninstrumental desires that concern physical items can be globally rational. (In light of the previous section, we already understand how there can be instrumental desires that concern physical items that are globally rational: we can desire a physical item such as chocolate as a means to get pleasurable sensations.) Surely it is natural to think that we do have noninstrumental desires that concern physical items that are globally rational. If a desire is globally rational, then the desire's possessor has a (nonrelative) reason for thinking that the object of the desire has value. And if the desire is also noninstrumental, then the reason will be a reason for thinking that the object of the desire has noninstrumental value. Now, many of us do think that there are physical items in the world that have noninstrumental value. Most of us reject hedonism; we think that there is more of (noninstrumental) value in the world than our pleasurable and painful mental states. And we take ourselves to be familiar with some of these extramental values; we take ourselves to have reason to think that certain physical items have value.

But recall the difficulty in understanding how (noninstrumental) desires that concern physical items can be globally rational (sec. 5.3). On my account, if a subject is to have a nonrelative reason for thinking that an item has value, she needs to stand in an intelligible relation to the item and its value. But how we can stand in intelligible relations to the values of physical items is not clear. Our rational desires have intelligible causes and so enable us to be intelligibly connected to those causes, but only mental states can be intelligible causes. So if we are to have globally rational desires that pertain to physical items, then somehow the mental states that are the intelligible causes of these desires must at the same time intelligibly connect us to the physical objects of these desires and their values. It is my aim in this section to explain how such a thing is possible.

Let's begin by looking at how I addressed the analogous problem that arose in connection with globally rational *beliefs* about the external world (sec. 4.4). There, too, to explain how beliefs about the external world could be globally rational, we needed mental states that could both function as intelligible causes of those beliefs and at the same time intelligibly connect us to the relevant parts of the external world. The mental states that could serve these functions were perceptual experiences: perceptual experiences can intelligibly cause beliefs, and at the same time experiences intelligibly connect us to parts of the external world, even though they are not intelligibly caused by states of the external world. Rather, perceptual experiences intelligibly connect us to parts of the external world because they have phenomenal properties that are intelligibly determined by observable properties of external objects. It is in virtue of these intelligible connections that we say that states of the external world reveal themselves to us in perceptual experience; it is in virtue of these intelligible connections that perceptual experiences count as *perceptions*. Similarly, we might think that what we need if we are to have globally rational desires are mental states that could constitute perceptions of *value*. Such mental states would both intelligibly cause desires that concern physical items, and would also have phenomenal properties that are intelligibly connected to the values of those physical items.

There is an obvious candidate for mental states that could constitute perceptions of value: feelings. The well-known idea that we perceive value in the world through our feelings has recently enjoyed renewed popularity.[20] I use the term "feelings" here to distinguish the mental states in question from (bodily) sensations; Michael Stocker (1983) has referred to these mental states as *psychic feelings* to emphasize this distinction. But feelings are also supposed to be similar in a certain way to sensations; I think we acknowledge this similarity when we characterize feelings as *affective* states (Johnston 2001). I will further characterize the nature of this similarity in what follows. Also, feelings are often thought to be related to emotions; sometimes feelings will be identified with emotions, whereas others claim simply that feelings are components of emotions.[21] Given this connection between feelings and emotions, we might also think of these feelings by which we perceive value in the world as our emotional reactions, or responses, to the world. Finally, the claim I am considering here is that the mental states that constitute perceptions of value are feelings; the claim is not that *all* feelings are perceptions of value. We have feelings that accompany our thoughts, actions, and imaginings that have nothing to do with perceiving value; the claim is merely that we have other feelings that do constitute perceptions of value.

Although I do wish to endorse this idea that we have feelings that constitute perceptions of value, we need to be careful about how we develop this idea. Although I want to argue that value properties (e.g., the property of being a good thing, the property of being a bad thing) can be perceived, I do not think we should say that they are perceived in the same way that typical observable properties such as colors, shapes, and sounds are perceived. As we have seen, there are phenomenal properties that are intelligibly determined by, and are therefore intelligibly similar to, observable properties of external objects (sec. 2.3, 2.4). But there are no phenomenal properties that are intelligibly similar to value properties; value properties are not perceived in such a direct manner, so to speak. In particular, the phenomenal properties of feelings are not intelligibly similar to value properties. The view that values do not exist, although mistaken, is at least a position that deserves to be taken seriously, whereas the comparable view about sensory properties such as colors and sounds does not.[22] I submit that we can explain the difference in terms of the different ways that sensory properties and value properties are perceived. Given the indirect way in which value properties are perceived, it is easy to be misled into thinking that they do not exist. I will argue that intelligible connections hold between the phenomenal properties of some of our feelings and the value properties of some physical items (in virtue of which these feelings can make our desires that concern these physical items globally rational), but we have not yet succeeded in characterizing the nature of these intelligible connections.

So what is the nature of these intelligible connections; how are value properties perceived? In trying to understand the way in which value properties are indirectly perceived, we need to keep in mind that value properties supervene on other kinds of properties. An object or event is not good or bad *simpliciter*; it is good or bad in virtue of certain of its properties. These are the properties on which the goodness or badness of the entity supervenes; they are the properties that *make* the entity good or bad. (More precisely, they make the entity good or bad *in certain respects*; an item can be good in certain respects and bad in others. I will ignore this complication in what follows.) I submit that if we are to perceive the goodness or badness of an entity, we need first to perceive the properties on which its goodness or badness supervenes.

Consider some physical object of value, whose value supervenes on its observable properties (a majestic mountain, for example). Suppose I am perceiving these observable properties; that is, I am having a perceptual experience in which I am conscious of these observable properties. What else needs to happen for me to perceive the value of these observable properties? My claim is that if I attend sufficiently to these observable properties, I become sensitive to the value of these properties, and I manifest this sensitivity by responding in a certain way to this value. Specifically, I respond *with feeling*; alternatively, I have an *emotional* response to the value of this object. Insofar as the feeling is a response to the value of the object, it counts as a *perception* of that value. I do not need first to believe that the object has value to respond to it with feeling; the feeling is a response to the value itself, not to some representation I might have of it. For example, I might look attentively at the mountain and be filled with awe, wonder, and amazement; I feel *thrilled*, say, but I feel thrilled *at* the sight of the mountain. The feeling is *directed* to, and is a response to, the mountain and its value; it is a perception of the majesty of the mountain.

What is the nature of these feelings that constitute perceptions of value, and in what sense are these feelings directed toward the physical objects we are perceiving? The feelings we are concerned with here just are a kind of perceptual experience with which we are already familiar. Recall that a perceptual experience consists in a subject engaged in an act of consciousness directed toward observable properties of an object of consciousness (sec. 2.3). When I am having a perceptual experience of a physical object of value and I respond to my consciousness of the observable properties on which the value supervenes by having certain kinds of feelings, I continue to have a perceptual experience of the object, but I am now perceiving the object *with feeling*. I am still conscious of the observable properties of the object, but my act of consciousness is now laden with feeling. Feelings are properties of acts of consciousness. The feelings we are concerned with here are *directed toward* the physical objects we are perceiving, in that these feelings are properties of acts of consciousness that are directed toward physical objects, acts of consciousness that are parts of perceptual experiences. As we noted earlier, not all feelings are perceptions of value, and so not all feelings will be parts of perceptual experiences. But all feelings will be properties of acts of consciousness; they are *ways* we are conscious of things, regardless of whether the things in question are physical objects, propositions, or something else.

(I am using the term "feelings" with two distinct senses. In one sense, "feelings" refers to certain properties of acts of consciousness. I sometimes refer to these properties as *feeling properties*. In another sense, the term refers to mental states that contain acts of consciousness that have feeling properties. Thus when I said in the previous paragraph that the feelings that constitute perceptions of value are a kind of perceptual experience, I was using the term in the latter sense. It should be clear from the context which sense of the term I am employing.)

We have begun to understand the sense in which certain kinds of feelings are perceptions of value, but we have not yet discovered the nature of the intelligible connections that hold between values and feelings. Let us now proceed to that task. I have argued that the feelings that constitute perceptions of value are perceptual experiences. But I have also argued that these feelings are *caused* by perceptual experiences, perceptual experiences in which we are conscious of observable properties that have value (observable properties on which value supervenes). The feelings are a response to our consciousness of, and attention to, these observable properties and their value. I now argue that these feelings are not mere responses to the perceptual experiences but intelligible responses to them. It is intelligible to respond to the consciousness of value with feeling. Perceptual experiences of observable properties on which value properties supervene have the intelligible power to cause certain kinds of feelings. The kinds of feelings that can be intelligibly caused by the perceptual experience will depend on the nature of the value properties associated with that experience. So, for example, whereas it is intelligible to respond to the majestic mountain with feelings of awe and amazement, it is intelligible to respond with repulsion in the face of a horrific crime.[23] In short, feelings are intelligibly connected with value in that perceptual experiences of observable properties with value can intelligibly cause certain kinds of feelings.

Why do I think that the causal connection here is an intelligible one, especially given that values and feelings are not (intelligibly) similar to each other? What is relevant here is that certain kinds of feelings *have* value. Just as there are pleasurable and painful bodily sensations, and the pleasurable sensations are good, and the painful sensations are bad, so too there are pleasurable and painful (i.e., unpleasant) psychic feelings, and the pleasurable feelings are good, and the painful feelings are bad. I think that what underlies the fact that perceptual experiences of observable properties with value can intelligibly cause certain kinds of feelings is the idea that it is intelligible to respond to good things by feeling good, and it is intelligible to respond to bad things by feeling bad. The world is filled with things of value, both good and bad, and it is not intelligible to feel nothing in the face of all this value. Such a blank response fails to appreciate the nature of this amazing thing called value. In the words of Max Scheler, "the value-qualities in value-affair-complexes *demand* certain qualities in emotional 'reactions of response' of the same type" ([1926] 1973, 258). Positive value ought to be celebrated, so to speak (and negative value mourned), and the way we celebrate value is through our emotional responses to it. A value-neutral world should be reacted to neutrally, but a value-laden world should be reacted to emotionally, with feeling. We are beings that are capable of being moved by things, and given that we *can* be moved, it is intelligible that we *are* moved by our confrontations with the value in the world. It is intelligible that we react to the perception of good things with positive feelings, and that we react to the perception of bad things with negative feelings. Note that the idea is not that these good things are good *because* they invoke positive feelings in us; neither are the bad things bad because they invoke negative feelings in us. On the contrary, positive feelings are supposed to be an intelligible response here because they are a response to something that is good independently of those feelings. Similarly, negative feelings are an appropriate response to something that is bad independently of those negative feelings.

We now understand how feelings intelligibly connect us to physical items and their values. But if feelings are to make desires (globally) rational, they also have to be intelligibly connected to desires; specifically, they have to be able to intelligibly cause desires. Feelings have these intelligible causal powers in virtue of their (intelligible) similarity to bodily sensations. Specifically, the sensational properties of bodily sensations are similar to the feeling properties of psychic feelings. We might say that both of these kinds of properties are kinds of feelings; when I have a bodily sensation, I have a feeling in some part of my body, whereas when I have a psychic feeling, it is literally my consciousness that feels a certain way (for feeling properties are properties of acts of consciousness). It is no accident that we use the word "feeling" to characterize both bodily sensations and psychic feelings; we use the same word here because sensational properties are similar to feeling properties. (Of course there are also differences; for example, there is a sense in which feeling properties are less intense than sensational properties.) Not only are sensational properties as a group similar to feeling properties as a group, however, but certain kinds of sensational properties are also similar in a more determinate way to certain kinds of feeling properties. In particular, as I already noted, just as there are pleasurable and painful bodily sensations, so too there are pleasurable and painful psychic feelings. And just as the pleasurable sensational properties are all similar to each other in a certain way, similarly, the pleasurable feeling properties are all similar to each other in a certain way, *and* the pleasurable feeling properties are similar in a certain way to the pleasurable sensational properties. Similar remarks apply to the painful feeling properties.

Given these similarities between pleasurable sensational properties and pleasurable feeling properties, pleasurable sensations and pleasurable feelings will have similar intelligible causal powers. Just as a pleasurable sensation can intelligibly produce a desire for the pleasurable sensation to continue, so too a pleasurable feeling can intelligibly give rise to a desire for the pleasurable feeling to continue. And just as a painful sensation can intelligibly produce a desire for the painful sensation to cease, similarly, a painful feeling can intelligibly give rise to a desire for the painful feeling to cease. Nevertheless there is an important difference between sensations and feelings that bears on their intelligible causal powers. Whereas sensational properties are properties of the *object* of consciousness, feeling properties are properties of the *act* of consciousness. These feeling properties will be *directed toward* the object of consciousness; in the cases with which we are concerned, cases in which the feelings are themselves perceptual experiences, the feeling properties will be directed toward a physical object, and toward the observable properties of the physical object on which its value supervenes. Since the feeling properties of the feeling are directed toward the object of consciousness, that is, since the feeling properties are in effect experienced as responses to the object of consciousness, the causal powers of the feeling that are intelligibly grounded in these feeling properties[24] will include the power to produce a noninstrumental desire that is itself directed toward the object of consciousness of the feeling. In other words, the feelings with which we are concerned will have the intelligible powers to produce not only desires that concern those very feelings but also (noninstrumental) desires that concern the physical objects that are the objects of those feelings. A pleasurable feeling (that constitutes a perception of value) will have the intelligible causal power to produce a desire for the feeling to continue, but it will also have the intelligible causal power to produce a desire for the physical object of the feeling to continue in existence. Similarly, a painful feeling (that constitutes a perception of value) will have the intelligible causal power to produce a desire for the feeling to cease, but it will also have the intelligible causal power to produce a desire for the physical object of the feeling to cease its existence. For example, when I am looking at the majestic mountain and am filled with feelings of awe and amazement at the sight of the mountain (and am thereby perceiving the value of the mountain), not only do I intelligibly want these wonderful feelings to continue, but I also intelligibly want the mountain itself to continue to exist. In virtue of my perception of the mountain's value, I have a reason for thinking that it would be a good thing for the mountain to continue to exist. My desire is not just rational but globally rational.

So there can be globally rational, noninstrumental desires that concern physical entities. Such desires are rational insofar as they are intelligibly caused by feelings.[25] Feelings are not propositional attitudes, and therefore no question arises about their own rationality. So a desire that is intelligibly caused by a feeling is not only rational but globally rational; the chain of justification can end with feelings. As we have also seen, when a subject has a desire that is globally rational, not only does he have a reason for thinking that the object of his desire has value, but he has a reason that intelligibly connects him to the object of his desire and its value. Feelings provide such reasons for us insofar as they can be intelligibly caused by perceptual experiences of properties on which value supervenes. Such feelings constitute perceptions of value. Pleasurable feelings provide us with perceptions of positive values, and painful feelings provide us with perceptions of negative values.

On my account, we can only perceive values that supervene on observable properties, and some might worry that this limitation puts too many values outside the range of perception. Perhaps some will think that only aesthetic-type values such as the majesty of a mountain will supervene on observable properties.

But I think that in fact a good many of the values we care about can be perceived. Consider the value of the activities in which we engage. It is important to us that we spend our lives engaged in worthwhile activities. And it is plausible to think that we can determine whether a given activity has value for us by participating in it and gauging our (emotional) reactions to it. John is considering whether to study to be a hospital nurse, but he doesn't know whether working in a hospital is really "for him." So John spends some time volunteering in a hospital to determine whether working in a hospital is for him. What John is trying to determine is whether working in a hospital would be a good way for him to spend his working life. The way John tries to determine this is by actually working in the hospital and seeing how he reacts to such work; in other words, he puts himself in a position where he is able to perceive the value of working in the hospital. If he reacts positively to the work, say, that would be a sign that the work has positive value for him. So suppose that John does react positively: he is engaged by working in the hospital, he is enthusiastic and excited about it, he enjoys it and derives pleasure from it. John is experiencing various positive, pleasurable feelings directed toward his work in the hospital; these positive feelings constitute his perception of the positive value of working in the hospital. He is able to perceive this value because it supervenes on observable properties of the activity of working in the hospital.[26]

Here is another example of a value that supervenes (at least in part) on observable properties: the value of human beings. I do not need to look into the soul of my ten-year-old daughter Emma to know her incomparable value; I just need to watch her. She has such a unique way of doing things and saying things, and when I take the time to attend to the things she does and the things she says and the way she does them and the way she says them, I am again filled with joy, wonder, and especially love at the amazing creature she is.[27]

I do not have a theory as to what kinds of values can be perceived and what kinds cannot. But I suspect that there is very little that is mysterious and hidden about the value in the world. It is right there on the surface; we need only be emotionally open to it.

Of course, it is not always easy to be open to the value in the world. Perceptual experiences of observable properties with value have the intelligible power to produce feelings in us that constitute perceptions of value. But this intelligible power is exercised only under certain conditions. These conditions do not obtain in a depressed person, for example. But even people able to experience feelings may not be open to the value in the world, for although feelings can be intelligibly caused by perceptual experiences of observable properties with value, they can also be caused in other ways. Suppose Joe has taken some mood-altering drug that puts him in a happy and excited mood. While in this mood, Joe goes on a first date with Jenny. Joe's mood causes him to experience various happy and excited feelings toward Jenny. Joe might even think that he is experiencing feelings of love toward Jenny, but we would be more inclined to describe his feelings as infatuation. Joe's feelings are not intelligibly caused by his attending to the observable properties of Jenny on which her value supervenes; rather, they are caused by his mood. His feelings are not perceptions of value but, in effect, hallucinations of value. His mood operates as a mask that prevents him from perceiving value. If we are to perceive the value in the world, it is not sufficient that we have feelings; we need to have feelings that are intelligibly responsive to the value in the world.

Joe's feelings toward Jenny might intelligibly produce in him a corresponding desire, say, a desire to spend more time with Jenny. Insofar as this desire is intelligibly caused, it is a rational desire. And given that the desire is rational, we can say that Joe has a reason for thinking that the object of his desire is good. But given that the feelings that intelligibly caused his desire are hallucinatory, the reason is fallible. Desires, like beliefs (sec. 3.3, 4.3), can be grounded in fallible reasons. Of course, it would be preferable if our desires were not grounded in fallible reasons. What is best is to be emotionally open to the values in the world, so that our desires can be intelligibly grounded in feelings that are genuine perceptions of value, feelings that are intelligibly responsive to the values in the world.

As the foregoing argument suggests, rationality is not the only standard that is applicable to desires. Desires, like beliefs (sec. 4.6), have an ideal form, and they are in this ideal form when they meet all the standards that apply to them. In the chapter's final section, I briefly examine what it takes for our desires to be ideal, and why this ideal is so important to us.

5.5 Ideal Desires: Consciousness and Value

At the end of chapter 4, I explained how the intrinsic nature of conscious belief is such as to determine certain standards for beliefs. Beliefs that meet these standards are *ideal* beliefs, and they qualify as knowledge. Similarly, the intrinsic nature of conscious desire is such as to determine certain standards for desires; desires that meet these standards are ideal desires.

Since beliefs and desires are both propositional attitudes, the standards that apply to desires parallel those that apply to beliefs. For example, just as an appropriateness standard applies to beliefs, so too an appropriateness standard applies to desires. Beliefs and desires are both kinds of *attitudes*, and so the question can arise with respect to both a belief and a desire as to whether the attitude is being held appropriately. Beliefs and desires that meet their respective standards of appropriateness are characterized as rational.

Beliefs and desires are also both subject to correctness standards. When I believe a proposition, I regard it as true, and I thereby represent it as true. The belief meets the correctness standard when the representation is correct, that is, when the proposition believed is true. Similarly, when I desire a proposition, I regard it as to be made true, and I thereby represent it as to be made true. The desire meets its correctness standard when its representation is correct, that is, when the desired proposition is made true. In other words, a desire is correct when it is satisfied. Satisfied desires parallel true beliefs in that both are propositional attitudes that have met their correctness standards.

Finally, both beliefs and desires are subject to a correspondence standard: that which makes the propositional attitude appropriate must explain why the propositional attitude is correct. In the case of beliefs, this translates into the idea that the reason the believer has for thinking that the proposition is true must explain why the proposition is true. Similarly, in the case of a subject's desire, the reason the subject has for thinking that the desire is to be satisfied must explain why the desire has been satisfied (i.e., made true).

Let us get clearer about the exact nature of this correspondence. The correspondence standard for desires requires that the reason that grounds a subject's desire explain why the desire has in fact been made true. But *how* can the reason that grounds a subject's desire explain why the desire has in fact been made true? Recall that a subject's reason for desiring is a reason for thinking that the object of desire is good (sec. 5.1). So if the subject's reason is to explain why the desire has in fact been satisfied, then it needs to be the case that the object of desire is in fact good, and that its goodness explains why the desire has been satisfied. But how exactly can the goodness of an object of desire explain why the desire has been satisfied (what is the mechanism, so to speak?). Well, here is one way that the goodness of a thing can explain how it comes to be made true. I perceive the value of something, and as a result I intelligibly have a desire concerning that thing, and I then act successfully to satisfy that desire. Here the goodness of the object of desire brings it about that the desire is satisfied in that my perception of the goodness of the object of desire leads me to satisfy the desire. So if a desire is to be ideal, not only must the desire be satisfied, and not only must the subject of the desire have a reason for thinking that the desired object is good, but the desired object has in fact to be good, and its goodness has to explain why the desire is satisfied.

We care about knowledge because knowledge is ideal belief, and it is important to us that we hold our beliefs in ideal form. Similarly, it is important to us that our desires be held in ideal form. We do not have a term that refers to ideal desires in the way that the term "knowledge" refers to ideal belief, but we manifest our interest in ideal desires in a variety of other ways. Perhaps it is obvious that we want our desires to meet the appropriateness and correctness standards, but we also want our desires to meet the correspondence standard. For example, consider the familiar idea that action will have moral value only if it is done for the right reason, that is, for the very reason that such action is morally required. I suggest that what underlies this familiar idea is the thought that it is not sufficient for morally good results to come about in the world; they need to come about *because* they are morally good. And the way morally good results can come about because they are morally good is for us to bring these results about for the very reason that we perceive them to be morally good. In other words, it is important to us that our desires to do what is morally required meet the correspondence standard. Similarly, with regard to desires in general, it is sometimes said that it is important that their satisfaction come about through our own efforts, and not through mere luck or happenstance. Again, our concern here is that our desires meet the correspondence standard: we want our desires to be satisfied through our own efforts because only through our own efforts can the value of the things we want actually operate to bring them about. Through our own efforts, we can perceive the value of the things we want and then work to achieve the things we want for the very reason that they have value.

Throughout this book, I have tried to explain the nature of consciousness in a way that highlights its value. I have discussed a variety of different kinds of conscious states, each important to us for different reasons. But desires have a special value for us, for they enable us to connect in an intimate way with the value of things other than consciousness. If our desires are to be ideal, not only must we have reason to think that the objects of our desires have value, and not only must these objects in fact have value, but we must satisfy our desires for the very reason that their objects have value.

The very nature of conscious desire commits us both to discovering the value already in the world (so as to make our desires appropriate) and to acting so as to bring new value into the world (so as to make our appropriate desires correct). The value of our desires is bound up with the value of things out there in the world, for if our desires are to be ideal and thus realize their ultimate value, then the objects of our desires must themselves have value, and we must realize this value by satisfying our desires. In this way, consciousness enables us to participate in the value of the world.

6 The Wonder of Consciousness: Conclusions

When consciousness appears in the world, something radically new comes into being. But the interest of consciousness does not lie in the addition of one more property to the long list of properties that are instantiated in the world. What is wonderful about consciousness is how it attaches itself to other properties in the world. It intelligibly relates us to the world and thereby enables the world to reveal itself to us.

In perceptual experience, we are conscious of various properties that are instantiated in the world, properties that thereby count as observable properties. These observable properties intelligibly combine with the acts of consciousness to which they are attached to produce in us new kinds of properties, phenomenal properties (sec. 2.3). I am conscious of a red surface, and lo and behold, there is something it is like for me to be conscious of that red surface. Phenomenal properties are the determinate ways we have of being conscious of the world. Consciousness does not merely bring one new property into the world; it brings many new properties into the world, one for each property in the world to which consciousness can attach itself.

The intelligibility of the way consciousness combines with observable properties to yield phenomenal properties is manifested in the intelligible similarities between phenomenal properties and their corresponding observable properties. There is an intelligible similarity between, say, the sensory redness of a surface and what it is like for me to be conscious of that redness. Phenomenal properties are intelligibly similar to their corresponding observable properties in that phenomenal properties just are observable properties instantiated in a special kind of way (sec. 2.4). The distinction between subjectivity and objectivity is the distinction between two different ways that properties can be instantiated. Consciousness is such a radically new phenomenon because it brings into the world a new way for properties to be instantiated.

Not only are phenomenal properties intelligibly similar to their corresponding observable properties, but phenomenal properties can be said to reveal the presence of their corresponding observable properties. The phenomenal properties of perceptual experiences intelligibly ground causal powers of these experiences to produce beliefs that the corresponding observable properties are instantiated (sec. 3.3). And not only does consciousness reveal to us observable properties of concrete, external objects, but it also reveals logical relations that hold between abstract objects. Perceptual experiences reveal portions of the concrete world to us, and rational intuitions reveal portions of the abstract world to us (sec. 3.5). And just as perceptual experiences can intelligibly produce beliefs about those portions of the concrete world that are revealed to us, so too rational intuitions can intelligibly produce beliefs about the revealed portions of the abstract world.

When consciousness reveals the world to us, we are passive with respect to the world. But consciousness also enables us to engage actively with the world, by means of consciously taking up attitudes toward propositions that represent the world. There are all kinds of attitudes we can take toward propositions, and the different attitudes we can take are just different ways we can be conscious of propositions (sec. 3.4). For example, we can consciously regard a proposition as being true (sec. 4.1), or we can consciously regard a proposition as to be made true (sec. 5.1).

With the advent of conscious propositional attitudes into the world, rationality makes its appearance in the world, as well, for only conscious propositional attitudes can be rational or irrational. The nature of certain kinds of attitudes is such as to give rise to the question as to whether it is appropriate to hold some particular attitude of that kind in a given context. In other words, certain kinds of attitudes determine standards of appropriateness for attitudes of that kind. For example, if I regard a proposition as being true, the question can arise as to whether it is appropriate for me to regard that proposition as being true (given that it is not up to me as to whether that proposition is true). A rational propositional attitude is a propositional attitude that is appropriately held. A propositional attitude is appropriately held when it is intelligibly caused. Only conscious states can be intelligible causes, so only conscious states can make propositional attitudes rational (sec. 4.1). Beliefs, for example, can be made rational (can be justified) by perceptual experiences, rational intuitions, and other beliefs.

The intrinsic conscious nature of a belief not only determines a standard of appropriateness for beliefs but determines other standards for beliefs as well. A belief that meets all the standards that apply to it counts as knowledge. Knowledge is the ideal form of conscious belief. Knowledge is so important to us because it is important to us that we be able to hold our beliefs in ideal form (sec. 4.6).

Desires have standards of appropriateness as well as beliefs. My desire for something is appropriate when I have reason to think that the object of my desire has positive value. It is because of our capacity to desire that we care so much about value, for it is important to us that our desires be appropriate (sec. 5.1). Desires can be made appropriate by feelings, for it is through our feelings that we perceive the value in the world (sec. 5.4).

Consciousness is different from everything else in the world, but it does not separate us from the world; on the contrary, it brings us into intelligibly intimate relations with the world. First the world is revealed to us through our experiences and rational intuitions of the world, and through our feelings toward the world. Then we in turn take up attitudes toward the world through our beliefs and desires, attitudes that give us an intimate stake in the ways the world is and the ways it could be.

Surely consciousness is a wonderful thing, and we are privileged to partake of it.

Notes

1   Introduction

1. A fact about a thing is *nonsubstantive* when the same fact is true of every other thing. So, for example, it is a nonsubstantive fact about that rock in front of me that it is identical to itself, because every object in the world is such that it is identical to itself. So the fact that the rock in front of me is identical to itself does not make that rock intelligible.

2. Throughout most of this chapter, I speak as if the intelligibility of consciousness is to be found solely in intelligible relations that hold between features of consciousness. In fact, I am simplifying here, so as not to unduly complicate matters at this early stage of the exposition. As I indicate toward the end of the chapter, I will also concern myself with intelligible relations that hold between features of consciousness and features of the world.

3. Hume famously argued that observation is needed to gain knowledge about any kind of causation, not just physical causation. See Hume's *Enquiry Concerning Human Understanding* (IV.i, VII.i) and his *Treatise* (I.iii.6). Hume's view is today the consensus view among philosophers (see chapter 3).

4. We are probably more accustomed to thinking of a justifiable conclusion as a proposition that stands in a relevant kind of *logical* or *rational* relation to the propositions we already know; similarly, we perhaps find it more natural to say that when we reason, we are searching for logical

or rational relations between propositions. But what determines whether relations between propositions are logical or rational? What determines, say, whether the conclusion of an inductive argument is logically or rationally related to the premises of the argument; what determines whether an inductive conclusion is *justified* by the premises from which it is inferred? In chapter 4, I argue that we need the idea of intelligibility to understand the relevant notions of rationality and justification.

5. In suggesting that logic is not a part of philosophy, I do not mean to make a substantive claim about the natures of logic and philosophy; disciplines are not the kind of thing to have such precise natures. Surely there are good reasons why logicians are to be found in philosophy departments, and I do not mean to dispute those reasons. But sometimes we do have occasion to distinguish logic from philosophy proper, because we are thinking of philosophy as a comparatively concrete a priori discipline, a discipline directly concerned with the nature of our lives in this concrete world. Philosophy is certainly interested in the nature of abstract entities such as propositions, numbers, and properties, but its interest in such items derives primarily from the nature of the relations those items stand in to concrete entities such as beliefs and particulars.

6. See, e.g., Locke's *Essay* (IV.i.5, IV.viii.8); Russell 1912, chap. 10; Chisholm 1977, 38–40; and BonJour 1998, chap. 4.

7. The locus classicus here is Hume; see, e.g., *Treatise* (I.iii.6, 86–87): "There is no object, which implies the existence of any other if we consider these objects in themselves, and never look beyond the ideas which we form of them. Such an inference wou'd amount to knowledge, and wou'd imply the absolute contradiction and impossibility of conceiving any thing different. But as all distinct ideas are separable, 'tis evident there can be no impossibility of that kind." For criticism of this "separability of distinct ideas" argument, see Stroud 1977, 47–52. Perhaps the most prominent contemporary denier of necessary connections is Lewis. Lewis defends what he calls "Humean supervenience . . . the doctrine that all there is to the world is a vast mosaic of local matters of particular fact, just one little thing and then another" (1986, ix).

8. A notable exception is Sprigge (1988, chap. 5; 1994). Sprigge claims that intelligible necessary relations hold between the categorical natures of pains and pleasures and their powers to cause certain kinds of behavior. I am sympathetic to Sprigge's claim and will defend a similar claim in chapter 5.

9. I am departing from the standard view of reductive physicalism, which holds that causal functionalism is not a version of reductive physicalism. (Kim [1998, 101] notes the standard view, although he disagrees with it himself.) One idea behind the standard view is that even if causal properties are actually realized by physical properties, they should not count as physical properties, so long as it is possible for the causal properties to be realized by nonphysical properties. I am counting causal properties that are (actually) realized by physical properties as physical properties, because on my view, the main dispute in the philosophy of mind is between those who hold that mental properties can be described with nonmental terminology and those who disagree, and I think that the terminology of reductionism and nonreductionism is best employed to characterize this dispute. Causal functionalism is reductionist in that it characterizes mental properties as causal properties and thus describes mental properties without employing mental terminology. Given that according to causal functionalism, these causal properties are realized by physical properties, there would seem to be no harm in characterizing these causal properties as physical properties, as well. We can also understand reductive physicalism to include teleological functionalism, which holds that mental properties are identical to teleological properties that are realized by physical properties. Teleological functionalists include Millikan (1984) and Dretske (1995).

10. Physicalists who deny the existence of nonreductive mental properties also have the option of denying the existence of mental properties altogether; in other words, instead of being reductive physicalists, they can be eliminative physicalists. Suffice it to say that few physicalists choose this option.

11. For further development of the idea that we have introspective knowledge that mental properties are something other than structural or causal properties, see McGinn 2004, 5–25. See also Lewis 1995. Lewis

is a reductive physicalist, and yet he acknowledges that reductive physicalism is incompatible with "folk psychology," for he holds that folk psychology includes the claim that we have introspective knowledge of the nonreductive essences of our mental properties.

12. For a small sample, see Block and Fodor 1972; Kripke 1980; Jackson 1982, 1986; and Chalmers 1996. Jackson (2004) rejects dualism and explains how he would respond to his prior argument for dualism.

13. Consider also the case of Chalmers. Chalmers is a dualist nonreductionist who clearly expresses his nonreductionism as follows: "Once we have explained all the physical structure in the vicinity of the brain, and we have explained how all the brain functions are performed, there is a further sort of explanandum: consciousness itself" (1996, 107). According to Chalmers, this further "explanandum is forced on us by first-person experience" (110). I take it that "first-person experience" is just another term for introspection. So although Chalmers portrays himself as providing a priori modal arguments for dualism, I submit that what really grounds his belief in dualism is his introspective evidence that consciousness is neither a structural nor a causal property.

14. I take this formulation of the argument from Papineau 1998, 375–376. It is clear from Papineau's discussion that the argument is intended to be not merely for physicalism but for reductive physicalism. We should understand references in the argument to physical causes and effects as referring only to reductive physical causes and effects. Also, Papineau explicitly notes that the argument's conclusion requires an identification of conscious *properties* with physical properties (376). An early version of the argument can be found in Lewis 1966.

15. For more detailed criticism of premise (3), see Marcus 2001. For additional criticism of premise (2), see Crane 1991 and Foster 1991, 198–201.

16. Armstrong makes the related claim that "perception of the secondary qualities involves an element of illusion" (1980, 31), for "although the secondary qualities *appear* to be simple, they are not in fact simple" (30; italics in original).

17. The idea that introspection does not inform us of the nature of mental properties was perhaps first suggested by Smart (1959, 149–150), who used the idea to respond to an objection to his physicalist identity theory. See also Armstrong 1980, 24–31. The idea has recently been revived by Loar (1997) and others who advocate the "phenomenal concept" strategy as a way to respond to antiphysicalist arguments. For discussions of the phenomenal concept strategy, see the articles collected in part 2 of Alter and Walter 2007.

18. Some physicalists claim that the commonsense belief in dualism results not from any putative introspective evidence (whether veridical or illusory) but from fallacious reasoning. See, e.g., Armstrong 1973, 189–191; Lycan 1987, 42–44, 77–78; Papineau 1993; Loar 1997, 609; and Jackson 2004, 430–432. These philosophers provide no support for their speculative claims about the etiology of the belief in dualism, and so I need not address their claims. For a brief discussion of Papineau's claim, see Langsam 2001, 400–401.

2   The Intelligibility of Consciousness I: How Experience Relates Us to the World

1. See, e.g., Smart 1959, 149–150; and Armstrong 1980, 24–31.

2. The proposition that colors have simple sensory natures is sometimes expressed by saying that "colors are sui generis"; the view is generally referred to as primitivism (Byrne and Hilbert 1997, xii). Byrne and Hilbert do not themselves subscribe to this view.

3. According to Armstrong (1973, 191), this mistake is responsible for "our introspective prejudice against Materialism": "Introspection and/or perception fails to indicate that the phenomenal qualities are both complex, and complexes of properties of the sort recognized by physics. The illusion must therefore be generated that these properties are simple and irreducible." Armstrong provides no evidence that such an illusion actually occurs and is the cause of our commonsense belief in nonreductionism. Also, he acknowledges that he "do[es] not think that this suggestion completely explains away the phenomenological implausibility of a purely Materialist theory of man" (ibid.).

4. Compare McGinn (1996), who apparently holds that colors are sensory properties (547), but also holds that they are not physical or mental properties (548).

5. Relevant passages in Hume are cited in note 3 of chapter 1. As I indicated there, I do not share the Humean view that no causal relations are intelligible relations. On the contrary, I argue in chapter 3 that some of the intrinsic features of conscious states do give rise to causal relations that are intelligible relations.

6. Representationalists include Harman (1990, 1996), Tye (1992, 1995, 2000), Dretske (1995), Lycan (1996), and Byrne (2001). Qualia theorists include Peacocke (1983), Boghossian and Velleman (1989), Block (1990, 1996), Stubenberg (1998), myself (2000), and Robinson (2004, chap. 4).

7. By contrast, representationalists just seem to deny that the world contains sensory properties. A. D. Smith (2002, 46) criticizes representationalism on this ground.

8. This kind of direct realism has recently been defended by McDowell (1982, 1986, 1994), myself (1997), Alston (1999), Johnston (2004), and Martin (2004, 2006). Snowdon (1981) does not defend direct realism, but he does a helpful job of elucidating the sense in which this kind of direct realism implies that the physical object one experiences is literally a part of one's experience.

9. This argument on behalf of qualia theory and against direct realism is a variation of the traditional arguments from hallucination and illusion in favor of sense-data theory. For a useful recent treatment of these arguments, see A. D. Smith 2002.

10. McDowell (1982, 1986, 1994), Martin (2004, 2006), and I (1997) are all direct realists who characterize ourselves as disjunctivists. For an excellent survey of the different kinds of disjunctivism and the arguments for and against disjunctivism, see Byrne and Logue 2009.

11. Arguments for the claim that conscious thoughts have phenomenal properties can be found in Strawson 1994, 5–13; 2005, sec. 6; Siewert 1998, chap. 8; and Pitt 2004.

12. Philosophers who cite the phenomenal differences between experiences and thoughts in arguing against representationalism include A. D. Smith (2002, chap. 1), Martin (2004, 39), Robinson (2004, chap.4), Siewert (2004, 33), and myself (2000).

13. I elaborate on this argument against Tye in Langsam 2000.

14. Consider Thau's account of the differences between perceptions and beliefs. According to Thau, "What distinguishes a belief that an object is red . . . from a perception according to which it *looks* red . . . [is] what they represent" (2002, 200). Specifically, the belief represents the color red, whereas the perception does not: it represents a property distinct from but corresponding to the color red. More generally, according to Thau, beliefs represent properties such as colors, shapes, sounds, et cetera, whereas perceptions do not represent any of these properties but instead represent properties that are distinct from but correspond to these properties (chap. 5). As far as I can understand Thau's view, these properties that correspond to the colors but are distinct from them are sensory properties, whereas Thau takes the colors themselves to be nonsensory properties. So Thau is saying that perceptions differ from beliefs in that perceptions represent sensory properties but do not represent nonsensory properties, whereas beliefs represent nonsensory properties but not sensory properties. The problem with this view is that we can believe what we perceive; our beliefs do represent sensory properties, for the very reason that our perceptual experiences represent these properties. My wife's dress instantiates the property of sensory redness. I can perceive the sensory color of her dress, and later at work, I can consciously believe that she will wear that dress, the dress with that sensory color, to the party tonight. John's criticism of Thau's view is similar; see John 2005, 171–172.

15. See also Jackson 2004, 434–435. Jackson similarly argues that nonconceptualism cannot account for the phenomenal differences between experiences and thoughts.

16. I am appealing here to what is traditionally known as the act-object conception of experience. Advocates of this view include Moore (1903), Russell (1911), Broad (1923, 252), and Price (1932); more recently the

view has been defended by Foster (2000) and Johnston (2004). See also Langsam 2002 for an exposition of this conception of experience. Advocates of the act-object conception typically come in two varieties: sense-data theorists and direct realists. Sense-data theorists hold that the act of consciousness in all experiences is directed toward a mental object, whereas direct realists such as myself hold that the act of consciousness in nonhallucinatory experiences is directed toward a physical object.

17. I remain neutral on the question of whether the demonstrative representational content is itself conceptual content. For the view that it is, see McDowell 1994, lecture 3. For criticism of McDowell's view, see, e.g., Kelly 2001 and Peacocke 2001.

18. I note that although Jackson (1977, 102–104), in opposition to my view, holds that the observable properties instantiated in experience are instantiated in sense data and not in physical objects, he nevertheless holds that these sense data are located in our familiar physical three-dimensional space. By contrast, Foster (2000, 157–160) holds the more traditional view that sense data are located in a nonphysical two-dimensional space. I confess that I do not understand why Foster adopts this view, or how Foster is able to explain how sense data *appear* to be in a three-dimensional space even though they are in fact located in a two-dimensional space.

19. I hope I have said enough earlier in this section about the nature of phenomenal externality to show that phenomenal externality cannot intelligibly be explained by the property of *representing* externality, that is, the property of representing there to be an external object. Remember that what needs to be explained here is how a multitude of observable property instantiations appear to have a certain kind of unity. Representational properties are properties of the *act* of consciousness (sec. 2.3), but what needs to be explained here is something about the instantiated observable properties to which the act of consciousness is *directed*. I fail to see how the mere act of representing these instantiated observable properties as properties of an external object can intelligibly result in these instantiated properties themselves *appearing* to be properties of an external object. Note that I am not denying that our experiences do typically represent the observable properties to be properties of

an external object; I am just denying that this representational property can intelligibly explain phenomenal externality. My point can also be expressed as follows. When I have a perceptual experience, and I represent with my act of consciousness that the instantiated observable properties to which my act of consciousness is directed are properties of an external object, then assuming that the property of phenomenal externality is instantiated in the experience, there will be something about the phenomenal character that makes it appear as if the representation is correct (there will be something about the phenomenal character that makes it appear as if the instantiated observable properties really are properties of an external object). But the representation itself cannot intelligibly explain why the representation appears to be correct. Therefore representationalism about phenomenal character fails to account for phenomenal externality (sec. 2.2).

3   The Intelligibility of Consciousness II: The Causal Powers of Conscious States

1. The question of whether laws of nature are brute or intelligible is distinct from the question of whether laws of nature are contingent or necessary. Even philosophers such as Shoemaker (1980, 1998) and Swoyer (1982) who hold that laws of nature are necessary nevertheless also hold that laws of nature are brute, in that they can be known only empirically.

2. Although we do not need laws of nature to *explain* the connection between an intelligible causal power and its underlying categorical property, we may still have reasons to acknowledge that laws of nature exist that *reflect* such intelligible connections. So if an intelligible explanatory connection holds between some causal power A and the categorical property B that grounds it, presumably there is still some sense in which a law of nature holds that conscious states with categorical property B have causal power A. This law of nature does not explain the existence of the connection between A and B; it merely reflects it.

3. I should acknowledge here that all the examples of intelligible causal powers that I consider in this book involve mental–mental causation.

For now, I remain neutral on the question of whether there are any examples of intelligible mental–physical causation.

4. Hume "affirm[s], as a general proposition, which admits of no exception, that the knowledge of this relation [i.e., the relation of cause and effect] is not, in any instance, attained by reasonings a priori; but arises entirely from experience, when we find that any particular objects are constantly conjoined with each other" (*Enquiry Concerning Human Understanding*, 27 [IV.i]).

5. Hume also purports to have a direct a priori argument that shows that we can have no a priori knowledge of causal powers; see *Treatise*, 86–87 (I.iii.6): "There is no object, which implies the existence of any other if we consider these objects in themselves, and never look beyond the ideas which we form of them. Such an inference wou'd amount to knowledge, and wou'd imply the absolute contradiction and impossibility of conceiving any thing different. But as all distinct ideas are separable, 'tis evident there can be no impossibility of that kind." See also *Enquiry Concerning Human Understanding*, 29–30 (IV.i). For decisive criticism of this "separability of distinct ideas" argument, see Stroud 1977, 47–52.

6. See *Enquiry Concerning Human Understanding*, VII.i.

7. Sprigge (1988, chap. 5; 1994) holds that pains and pleasures have intelligible causal powers. See also O'Shaughnessy 2000, 496–497; and Hawthorne 2004, 355; these authors also seem to be suggesting that there are mental states that have intelligible causal powers.

8. The notion of acquaintance is most closely associated with Russell; see, e.g., Russell 1911. Contemporary philosophers who defend a Russellian notion of acquaintance include McDowell (1986) and Fumerton (1995). A well-known defender of the traditional idea of the given is Price (1932, chap. 1); for contemporary defenses of this idea, see Fales 1996 and BonJour 2003a, chap. 4.

9. The seminal attack on the "myth" of the given is Sellars 1963. More recent criticism of the idea of the given can be found in BonJour 1985, chap. 4; and McDowell 1994, lecture 1.

10. See, e.g., Jackson 1982, 133; and Chalmers 1996, 151–152, 159. Note that although Chalmers expresses sympathy with epiphenomenalism, he does not subscribe to the view himself.

11. I am not claiming that we find epiphenomenalism to be logically contradictory. Although I am claiming that we have a priori knowledge of some of the causal powers of some of our conscious states, the knowledge at issue is *synthetic*, not analytic, and so it is not a consequence of my view that epiphenomenalism is a logical contradiction. By contrast, (analytic) functionalism holds that we have a priori *analytic* knowledge of some of the causal powers of our mental states, and therefore it is a consequence of functionalism that epiphenomenalism is a logical contradiction. But epiphenomenalism does not seem to us to be a logical contradiction, and so functionalism faces an objection that my own view avoids. I discuss functionalism further later in the chapter.

12. I am thinking here especially of the familiar objection that functionalist analyses leave out the phenomenal character of experiences. See, e.g., Block and Fodor 1972.

13. Contemporary philosophers who accept a priori synthetic knowledge include Chisholm (1977, chap. 3) and BonJour (1998).

14. Price 1932, 7. Price's claim that a subject can think about something only if it is brought before the subject's mind is basically equivalent to "Russell's principle," which holds that "every proposition which we can understand must be composed wholly of constituents with which we are acquainted" (Russell 1912, 58). A useful discussion of Russell's principle can be found in Evans 1982, 89–120.

15. The notion of attention under discussion here is helpfully elucidated by Martin (1997, 78): "Arguably, it is part of the manifest image of the mind that we are aware of objects of sense experience in a different way from being aware of the objects of thought, and that this is reflected in the ways attention can relate one to an object of sense as opposed to thought. . . . It is tempting to think of experience in terms of a whole array of items stretching beyond what I have focused my attention on at a time—an array over which I could move my attention, as a beam or spotlight. It is as if I am aware of the whole array at a time, albeit more

or less determinately, whether I now focus my attention on one part of it or not; and my awareness of some element of it can explain why I shift my attention from one part of the scene to another. There seems to be no corresponding array of items to shift one's attention over in thought: if we think of thoughts as determinations of attention, then there can be no way of thinking of something without thereby to some extent to be attending to it." See also Martin (1998, 171): "We can attend to objects that we perceive in ways not present when merely thinking about them. . . . In perception, focal attention seems to range over objects which are already objects of awareness, and a motive for directing your attention to something is to find out more." Feldman (2004, 216–218) has recently emphasized the importance of attention as a necessary condition for the epistemic justification of foundational beliefs.

16. I address the question of how a subject becomes able to attend to phenomenal properties in section 3.6.

17. See Martin's suggestion that we think of thoughts as "determinations of attention" (1997, 78).

18. In fact, I need to make a qualification here. There are some observable properties such that attention to the property must be supplemented by another factor for the belief that the property is instantiated to be intelligibly formed. Consider the hen's observable property of having forty-three speckles, for example. Mere attention to the speckles on the part of a subject will not suffice to enable the subject to intelligibly form the belief that the hen has forty-three speckles; in addition, the subject must count the speckles. This note constitutes the beginning of a response to Sosa's "speckled hen" argument against internalist foundationalism (2003, chap. 7).

19. I should say more precisely that what a subject can *directly* attend to is determined by the phenomenal character of the experience. As I explain in the text, in both veridical and hallucinatory experiences, the subject can (directly) attend to instantiations of observable properties that appear unified in a certain way. In the case of a nonhallucinatory experience, the observable properties are in fact instantiated in an exter-

nal object, and the subject can (indirectly) attend to this external object by attending to its observable properties (sec. 3.3.1). In the case of a hallucinatory experience, on the other hand, the instantiated observable properties are not instantiated in an external object, and therefore the subject cannot attend to an external object. So even when a veridical experience and a hallucinatory experience share the same phenomenal character, the objects of indirect attention will differ, though the objects of direct attention will be the same. I will generally ignore this distinction between direct and indirect attention in what follows.

20. The objector here echoes the concerns of Carroll (1895).

21. Cf. Harman (1986, 5): "Consider again modus ponens. This principle does not say that, if one believes P and also believes *if P then Q*, then one can infer Q, because that is not always so. Sometimes one should give up P or *if P then Q* instead."

22. The subject might have both these intelligible powers in the sense that it might be intelligible for the subject *either* to acquire the belief that q *or* to give up the belief that p. But it might not be intelligible for the subject to exercise both these causal powers simultaneously.

23. For recent discussions of rational intuition, see Bealer 1996a, 123–124; 1996b, 168–169; and BonJour 1998, chaps. 4 and 5. Bealer emphasizes that rational intuitions are not beliefs. He also suggests that rational intuitions are akin to perceptual experiences, in that he characterizes them as "a kind of seeming, namely intellectual seeming" (1996b, 168). See also Plantinga's discussion of the phenomenology that accompanies a priori knowledge (1993, 103–108), and Fumerton's discussion of states of direct acquaintance with logical relations (1995, chap. 7).

24. Given that rational intuitions are similar to experiences with respect to their phenomenal properties, we might wonder whether there exist "hallucinatory" rational intuitions comparable to hallucinatory experiences. BonJour (1998, chaps. 4 and 5) holds that rational intuitions are fallible, which seems to imply that there are hallucinatory (rational) intuitions. A hallucinatory experience is an experience in which the property of phenomenal externality is instantiated but the property of

externality is not (sec. 2.5). In other words, it is an experience in which the property of externality is instantiated in the special phenomenal way without being instantiated in the standard nonphenomenal way. So presumably a hallucinatory intuition that p entails q would be an intuition in which the relation of entailment obtains between p and q in the special phenomenal way without obtaining between them in the standard nonphenomenal way. But I am not clear that I can make sense of the idea of an intuition of this kind. It seems to me definitive of an experience-like conscious state (as opposed to, say, a conscious propositional attitude) that it enables its subject to attend to instantiations of some nonphenomenal, nonrepresentational property (sec. 3.3). A hallucinatory experience counts as an experience because its subject, although not able to attend to (standard) instantiations of the property of externality, is able to attend to instantiations of observable properties that appear unified in a certain way (sec. 3.3.3). But I cannot see that there is any nonphenomenal, nonrepresentational property to which a subject undergoing a hallucinatory intuition that p entails q would be able to attend. Therefore I am not yet ready to affirm the existence of hallucinatory intuitions. It seems to me that BonJour affirms the existence of hallucinatory intuitions because he thinks that he needs them to account for the fallibility of our a priori beliefs. If I ultimately reject the existence of hallucinatory intuitions, then I would need to give an alternative account of the fallibility of our a priori beliefs. Such an alternative account should be possible, for as I noted at the beginning of this section, not all beliefs that are produced by reflection are caused by rational intuitions. But I do not have such an alternative account at the present time. Nor am I now in a position to come down one way or another on the question of the existence of hallucinatory intuitions. I hope to address these issues at a later time.

25. See Shoemaker 1994, 254–255: "No one thinks that in being aware of a sensation or sensory experience one has yet another sensation or experience that is 'of' the first one, and constitutes its appearing to one in a particular way. No one thinks that one is aware of beliefs and thoughts by having sensations or quasi-sense-experiences of them."

26. My discussion in this paragraph is inspired by Moore's remarks about the difficulties of attending to acts of consciousness (1903, 446,

450): "When we refer to introspection and try to discover what the sensation of blue is, it is very easy to suppose that we have before us only a single term. The term 'blue' is easy enough to distinguish, but the other element which I have called 'consciousness'—that which the sensation of blue has in common with the sensation of green—is extremely difficult to fix. That many people fail to distinguish it at all is sufficiently shown by the fact that there are materialists. . . . The moment we try to fix our attention upon consciousness and to see *what*, distinctly, it is, it seems to vanish: it seems as if we had before us a mere emptiness. When we try to introspect the sensation of blue, all we can see is the blue: the other element is as if it were diaphanous. Yet it *can* be distinguished if we look attentively enough, and if we know that there is something to look for."

4 The Importance of Consciousness I: Belief, Rationality, and Knowledge

1. See, e.g., McGrew 1995, 8–10; and BonJour 2003b, 174–177. Cohen (1984) argues more generally for a connection between epistemic justification and truth.

2. We do speak of having standing propositional attitudes that are not always present to consciousness, but since I am concerned here with conscious mental states, I set aside the questions of whether we can make sense of such talk of standing propositional attitudes and, if so, how best to do so.

3. We can distinguish two kinds of intelligible causation here. An attitude can be intelligibly caused either (1) by being intelligibly *produced*, in that the cause intelligibly determines the initial acquisition of the attitude, or (2) by being intelligibly *sustained*, in that the cause intelligibly determines that the attitude continues to be held after its initial acquisition. I claim that an attitude can be appropriately held either by being intelligibly produced or by being intelligibly sustained. For example, suppose we can make sense of the idea of a belief that is stored in memory in an unconscious form when it is not present to consciousness (see previous note). Now consider a belief of this type that is not being

causally sustained in an intelligible way; suppose, say, that the belief is stored in memory, but its supporting evidence has been forgotten. Nonetheless it might be rational and appropriate to continue to hold this belief insofar as the belief was initially causally produced in an intelligible way. Here I mean to echo the idea that causal requirements for epistemic justification can be met either by causal production or by causal sustainment; see, e.g., Goldman 1979, 8–9. (I discuss the connection between epistemic justification and intelligible causation in section 4.5.) When discussing intelligible causation in chapter 3, I sometimes focused specifically on intelligible production. But in fact the same considerations I adduced to explain how certain mental states can intelligibly produce beliefs would also apply to explain how these same mental states can intelligibly sustain beliefs. From here on in, my talk of intelligible causation should be understood to include both intelligible production and intelligible sustainment.

4. This view of rationality seems to be implied by such varied philosophers as Sellars (1963), Rorty (1979, chaps. 3 and 4), BonJour (1985), and Davidson (1986).

5. See, e.g., BonJour's attempt to provide "a reasonable outline of the concept of coherence" (1985, 93).

6. For Hume's discussion of induction, see his *Enquiry concerning Human Understanding*, IV and V.

7. If BonJour is correct in arguing that inductive inference can be justified a priori (1998, chap. 7), then presumably his argument could be supplemented to show that beliefs formed by inductive inference can be intelligibly caused. I will not address BonJour's argument at this time.

8. Similarly, the question of whether explanatory inference (inference to the truth of a conclusion on the grounds that it is the best explanation of the premises) is rational should be understood as the question of whether beliefs formed by explanatory inference are intelligibly caused. For the view that inductive inference just is a kind of explanatory inference, see Harman 1965.

9. For recent formulations of arguments for external-world skepticism, see, e.g., Stroud 1984, chap. 1; Brueckner 1994; Cohen 1998; and Pritchard 2005.

10. The notion of tentative acceptance can be found in Harman 1986, 46–50.

11. Perhaps there are also notions of appropriateness and rationality applicable to beliefs other than the two I have described. Thus some would say that my holding some belief is *instrumentally* rational (or pragmatically rational, or prudentially rational) if holding that belief is a means to satisfy some desire of mine. I have no problem in acknowledging such other notions of rationality. Nevertheless I would argue that the two standards of rationality for beliefs that I have described have a certain kind of primacy. These two standards are derived solely from the intrinsic nature of belief: as I argued earlier, given only the fact that for a subject to believe p is for the subject to regard p as true, the question arises as to whether it is appropriate for the subject to regard p as true (sec. 4.1). The notion of appropriateness invoked here is either global or local appropriateness. To invoke other standards of appropriateness, we must appeal to standards extrinsic to the nature of belief. Consider the notion of instrumental rationality referred to earlier. If we limit ourselves only to the consideration of facts about the nature of belief, we have no reason to think that whether a belief is a means to satisfy a desire has anything to do with whether that belief is rational and appropriate. Only facts about the nature of desire suggest there may be something appropriate about satisfying desires (sec. 5.5).

12. Cf. Goldman 1979, 15. Goldman considers a subject S with a set of beliefs B, some of which are unjustified. S then employs a "sound" reasoning procedure to infer from the entire set B to the conclusion that p, and thereupon believes that p. Goldman acknowledges that there is a sense in which S's belief that p is justified.

13. See BonJour 1985, 91: "The epistemic issue on a particular occasion will usually be merely the justification of a single empirical belief, or a small set of such beliefs, within the context of a cognitive system whose

overall justification is (more or less) taken for granted; we may call this the *local* level of justification."

14. Harman (1986, 46) proposes a "principle of conservatism" for beliefs and intentions according to which "one is justified in continuing fully to accept something in the absence of a special reason not to." Chisholm (1982, 14) advocates the "principle that *anything* we find ourselves believing may be said to have *some* presumption in its favor—*provided* it is not explicitly contradicted by the set of other things we believe" (italics in original).

15. For discussions of the epistemic regress argument, see, e.g., BonJour 1985, chap. 2; and Audi 2003.

16. The phrase originated with Sellars (1963).

17. See BonJour 1978; 1985, chap. 4. BonJour has since changed his view and has accepted the legitimacy of noninferential justification; see BonJour 1999, 2003a.

18. For coherentism, see, e.g., Lehrer 1974 and BonJour 1985. Goldman (1979) introduced (process) reliabilism; for further elaborations of the view, see, e.g., Goldman 1986 and Alston 1995. Other externalist accounts can be characterized as versions of reliabilism, insofar as they include reliability as a necessary requirement for knowledge; consider, e.g., Plantinga's proper functionalism (1993, 17–21), Greco's agent reliabilism (2000, chap. 7), and Sosa's virtue epistemology (2003, chap. 9).

19. One might object that all my argument shows is that intelligible causation is a necessary condition of justification, and therefore I should allow for the possibility of hybrid views of justification, such as the view that a belief would have to be both intelligibly and reliably caused to be justified. I do not have any knockdown arguments against such hybrid views, but I fail to see any rationale for them. Once it is realized that a justified belief needs to be an appropriately held belief and therefore an intelligibly caused belief, there seems to be no reason to impose any additional requirements on justified beliefs. See also my argument in section 4.6 relating to the requirements for knowledge.

20. For similar characterizations of internalism, see, e.g., Fumerton's discussion of "internal state" internalism (1995, 60–62), Sosa's discussion of "ontological internalism" (1999, 149), and Conee and Feldman's discussion of "mentalism" (2001, 232–236).

21. See, e.g., BonJour 1985, chaps. 1 and 3; 2003a; 2003b; Alston 1986; Plantinga 1990; Goldman 1999; Sosa 1999, 2003; and Steup 1999.

22. See Korcz 1997, 171: "The standard view is that the correct analysis of the basing relation will be some sort of causal analysis." A notable dissenter to this standard view is Lehrer (1974, 122–126), but I agree here with Goldman (1979, 22n8), who insists that Lehrer's putative counterexample to the standard view is unconvincing. For an example of a causal analysis of the basing relation, see Moser 1989, 156–158.

23. Consider, for example, a subject's experience of maroon. A subject's experience of maroon has the power to intelligibly cause the subject to believe that the object of the experience is maroon. But this intelligible causal power will be exercised only if the subject is sufficiently attending to the instantiated maroon of the object of experience (sec. 3.3.2). Sufficient attention to the instantiation of the property of maroon is a necessary initiating *condition* for the exercise of the experience's causal power.

24. Williamson 2000, 1. I should note that the interpretation I am giving to these remarks of Williamson is very different from Williamson's own understanding of them. Thus my using these remarks to develop my own account of knowledge should not indicate any agreement with Williamson's views about knowledge. Specifically, Williamson holds that the concept of knowledge is unanalyzable, whereas my purpose here is precisely to give an analysis of the concept of knowledge. I will not be examining Williamson's views in this book.

25. Although we can distinguish two standards of appropriateness for beliefs, given that global rationality entails local rationality, I will continue to speak somewhat loosely of *the* appropriateness standard for beliefs.

26. I leave it to the reader to verify this claim. But consider just one well-known Gettier counterexample. "Take the case in which I have

strong evidence that Nogot, who is in my class, owns a Ford, no evidence that anyone else does, but Havit, who is also in my class, owns a Ford, quite unknown to me, and Nogot does not. I do not know that someone in my class owns a Ford" (Lehrer 1979, 74). I lack knowledge here because my belief that someone in my class owns a Ford fails to meet the correspondence standard: my reason for thinking it is true that someone in my class owns a Ford does not explain why it is in fact true that someone in my class owns a Ford. My reason for thinking it is true that someone in my class owns a Ford is a reason for thinking it is true that Nogot owns a Ford. But since Nogot does not own a Ford (Havit does), my reason for thinking it is true that someone in my class owns a Ford does not in fact explain why someone in my class owns a Ford. My belief fails to meet the correspondence standard, and therefore I lack knowledge.

5   The Importance of Consciousness II: Desire, Feeling, and Value

1. See Velleman 1992, 11: "The propositional object of desire is regarded not as fact—not, that is, as *factum*, having been brought about—but rather as *faciendum*, to be brought about; it's regarded not as true, but as to be made true." See also M. Smith 1994, 7: "On the one hand there are beliefs, states that purport to represent the way the world is. . . . On the other hand, there are desires, states that represent how the world is to be." Velleman remains neutral as to what it is about propositional attitudes that confers on them their particular attitudes (1992, 23n16), whereas Smith gives a functional account of the attitudes (1994, 111–116). By contrast, I am arguing that the intrinsic nature of its act of consciousness determines the attitude of a propositional attitude (sec. 3.4). I should also note that this difference in attitude between beliefs and desires is sometimes referred to as a difference in their "direction of fit"; for more on the idea of direction of fit, see, e.g., Searle 1983, as well as the aforementioned works by Velleman and Smith.

2. Velleman argues that it is *impossible* to desire the unattainable (1992, 16–17), whereas I make the weaker claim that it is merely inappropriate and irrational to do so. From the fact that it is impossible for some proposition to be made true, it does not follow that it is impossible for

me to regard that proposition as to be made true. The past cannot be changed, but nevertheless I can want it to be the case that the past is different in some way. My father died last year, and I know that fact cannot be changed, but nevertheless I can genuinely want it to be the case that my father had not died last year. Such a desire is irrational, but given my grief, that I might have such a desire is nevertheless understandable. On the other hand, there is nothing irrational or inappropriate about my merely *wishing* that my father had not died last year. As I note in the text, wishing is a different kind of propositional attitude than desiring (Velleman 1992, 17) and therefore has different standards of appropriateness.

3. See Hume's *Treatise* (II.iii.3); see also, e.g., M. Smith's reference to "Hume's claim that desires are themselves beyond rational criticism" (1994, 14).

4. Cf. Anscombe 1963, viii: "If a man wants something, he can always be asked what for, or in what respect it is desirable; until he gives a desirability characterization."

5. Cf. Velleman 1992, 11: "To desire something is to be disposed toward it in a way that would be appropriate if the thing were good."

6. Thus I oppose philosophers who hold that to desire something *is* to regard it as being good; such philosophers include Anscombe (1963, 76), Stampe (1987, 355), and Helm (2001, 81–89). I oppose these philosophers because I think that it is possible to desire something that one regards as bad; here I follow Velleman (1992). Stocker (1979) argues that it is not only possible but commonplace to desire the bad; Velleman (1992, 17–18) endorses Stocker's conclusions and notes that they support the denial of the view that to desire something is to regard it as good. Helm (2001, 84) claims that if you deny that to desire something is to regard it as good, then you are not entitled to hold that it is inappropriate to desire the bad. I believe that I have shown in the text why Helm's claim is mistaken.

7. The difficulties of making sense of practical inference are discussed by, among others, Stampe (1987, 335–342); and Schueler (1995, 101–102).

8. See, e.g., M. Smith 1994, 147–151.

9. Philosophers who hold that desires provide reasons for action include Williams (1979), Nagel (1986, 166–171), Stampe (1987, 342–348), and Schueler (1995, 110–114). Philosophers who deny this claim include Scanlon (1998, 41–49) and Brewer (2002, 467–473). Specifically, Scanlon argues that "when we consider the various states that might be identified as desires we find none that can play the general role in justification commonly assigned to desires—that of states which are independent of our practical reasoning and which, when they occur, provide reason for doing what will promote their fulfillment" (1998, 49).

10. As I noted earlier (chap. 3, n. 3), in this book I remain neutral on the question of whether there are any examples of intelligible mental–physical causation. Thus I remain neutral on the specific question of whether desires (or intentions) can intelligibly cause actions. My point here is merely that those who hold that desires are reasons for action are committed to the view that desires can intelligibly cause actions. I acknowledge that I am sympathetic to the view that desires can intelligibly cause actions, but I will not argue for it here.

11. I mean to distinguish the claim that I refer to here as internalism from the view that gets discussed under that name in the literature, and I leave open the question of how these two views are related. Internalism was first formulated and defended by Williams, who talked of reasons needing to be relative to the "agent's *subjective motivational set*" (1979, 102; italics in original), which can contain, in addition to desires, "such things as dispositions of evaluation, patterns of emotional reaction, personal loyalties, and various projects, as they may be abstractly called, embodying commitments of the agent" (105). Thus Williams's view is apparently less restrictive than the view I discuss, the view that only desires can provide reasons for action. But Schueler (1995, 54–57) argues that internalism avoids triviality only if it holds that only desires can be reasons for action. Similarly, Millgram (1996, 208–209) argues that the internalist should not interpret the notion of a subjective motivational set in an expansive manner; for that reason, Millgram characterizes internalism as the view that "someone's reason for doing something has to bottom out in what that person wants" (197). I am

sympathetic with the arguments of Schueler and Millgram, but I will not say anything further here about the issue they are addressing. My concern here is to evaluate the view that only desires can be reasons for action; I leave aside the question of how this view relates to Williams's view.

12. Externalists include McDowell (1995), Millgram (1996), and Brewer (2002).

13. Nevertheless some will perhaps suggest that rational intuitions can intelligibly cause desires by means of intelligibly causing evaluative beliefs, for if truths about value are necessary truths, perhaps we can rationally intuit some of these necessary truths. I am undecided as to whether to endorse this suggestion, so I will not pursue it any further here.

14. Helm (2001, 90) remarks similarly about the connection between pain and behavior: "Pains do not simply cause us to behave in certain ways; they rationally motivate such behavior."

15. Here I am following Sprigge (1988), who holds that pains and pleasures are intelligible causes of behavior. Specifically, Sprigge claims that "pleasure and pain are distinct qualities of experience which necessarily tend to influence behaviour in certain ways" (148). Sprigge clearly intends for this necessity to be an intelligible one, for he takes his position to involve a rejection of Hume's "denial of intelligible necessities in nature," and a commitment to the view that "reality is intelligible, and that it is of the nature of certain sorts of things to exert a certain sort of influence in the world" (141). My position here is weaker than Sprigge's, as I claim only that pains and pleasures are intelligible causes of desires, not behavior. As I noted earlier, I wish to remain neutral on the question of whether desires can intelligibly cause behavior.

16. Entities such as pains and pleasurable sensations can be good in certain respects and bad in others; they can have both good and bad *aspects*. In referring to the badness of pain, I am referring to the bad *aspect* of pain, and similarly, when I refer to the goodness of pleasurable sensations, I am referring to the good *aspect* of such sensations. I am concerned in this section with the bad aspect of pains and the good

aspect of pleasurable sensations; I allow that pains may also have good aspects, and pleasurable sensations may also have bad aspects.

17. Again, I am following Sprigge here: "Pleasantness is a generic quality of which different pleasures are specific forms. Pleasure is related to the specific sorts of pleasure somewhat as colour is related to the various shades of colour (or red to the various shades of red). Just as colour can only be exemplified in some specific version, so with pleasure" (1988, 137).

18. Similarly, if I have no desire to prolong an intensely pleasurable but relaxing massage, this circumstance is no counterexample to my claim that pleasurable sensations have the intelligible causal power to produce desires for the sensations to continue. The example can be found in Rachels (2000, 192, 201), who employs it to argue against Sprigge's (1988) view that pains and pleasures are intelligible causes of certain characteristic kinds of behavior. As I explained in note 15, Sprigge's view seems to be stronger than my own; even if the example succeeds as a counterexample to Sprigge's view, it does not succeed as a counterexample to my own.

19. This view has been defended by Rachels (2000), who methodically criticizes a variety of opposing views. I have nothing to add here to Rachels's criticisms.

20. See, e.g., Scheler [1926] 1973, 35: "Values are given first of all in feeling." More recent defenders of the view that some feelings constitute perceptions of value include Millgram (1993), Helm (2001), Johnston (2001), de Sousa (2002), and Kupperman (2005).

21. Helm (2001, 33) identifies emotions with feelings of a certain kind, whereas Goldie (2000) argues that feelings are components of emotions. For a contrary view, see Johnston 2001, 182n1; Johnston claims that the feelings that constitute perceptions of value are not emotions. For a response to Johnston, see Wedgwood 2001, 215n1.

22. The view that values do not exist is defended by Mackie (1977).

23. The example of feeling repulsed by a horrific crime is Johnston's (2001); he characterizes the feeling of repulsion as an "*appropriate* affect" (193; italics mine). My account explains why the affect is appropriate.

24. Strictly speaking, the causal powers in question will be intelligibly grounded in the phenomenal properties of the feeling that are determined by the feeling properties.

25. Johnston speaks of how "the presence of the affect can make the desire or action especially intelligible to the agent himself. It can make the desire or act seem apt or fitting in a way that silences any demand for justification" (2001, 189). But Johnston does not appeal to the idea of intelligible causation, so he is unable to explain how an affect makes a desire intelligible.

26. See also Millgram 1993, 394–397, for a useful discussion of some other cases in which we learn the value of activities on the basis of the feelings we have when we engage in such activities.

27. See also Gaita's (2000, 29–55) remarks on how we are able to obtain knowledge of the value of human beings through feelings of grief and remorse.

References

Alston, W. 1986. Internalism and externalism in epistemology. Rept. in his *Epistemic Justification*, 185–226. Ithaca: Cornell University Press, 1989.

Alston, W. 1995. How to think about reliability. *Philosophical Topics* 23:1–29.

Alston, W. 1999. Back to the theory of appearing. In *Philosophical Perspectives*, vol. 13, *Epistemology*, ed. J. Tomberlin, 181–203. Malden, Mass.: Blackwell.

Alter, T., and S. Walter, eds. 2007. *Phenomenal Concepts and Phenomenal Knowledge: New Essays on Consciousness and Physicalism*. New York: Oxford University Press.

Anscombe, G. E. M. 1963. *Intention*. Ithaca: Cornell University Press.

Armstrong, D. M. 1968. *A Materialist Theory of the Mind*. London: Routledge & Kegan Paul.

Armstrong, D. M. 1973. Epistemological foundations for a materialist theory of mind. *Philosophy of Science* 40:178–193.

Armstrong, D. M. 1980. *The Nature of Mind*. St. Lucia, Queensland: University of Queensland Press.

Audi, R. 2003. Contemporary modest foundationalism. In *The Theory of Knowledge: Classical and Contemporary Readings*, 3rd ed., ed. L. Pojman, 174–182. Belmont, Calif.: Wadsworth.

Bealer, G. 1996a. *A priori* knowledge and the scope of philosophy. *Philosophical Studies* 81:121–142.

Bealer, G. 1996b. *A priori* knowledge: Replies to Lycan and Sosa. *Philosophical Studies* 81:163–174.

Block, N. 1990. Inverted earth. In *Philosophical Perspectives*, vol. 4, *Action Theory and Philosophy of Mind*, ed. J. Tomberlin, 53–79. Atascadero, Calif.: Ridgeview.

Block, N. 1996. Mental paint and mental latex. In *Philosophical Issues*, vol. 7, *Perception*, ed. E. Villanueva, 19–49. Atascadero, Calif.: Ridgeview.

Block, N., and J. A. Fodor. 1972. What psychological states are not. *Philosophical Review* 81:159–181.

Boghossian, P., and J. D. Velleman. 1989. Colour as a secondary quality. *Mind* 98:81–103.

BonJour, L. 1978. Can empirical knowledge have a foundation? *American Philosophical Quarterly* 15:1–13.

BonJour, L. 1985. *The Structure of Empirical Knowledge*. Cambridge, Mass.: Harvard University Press.

BonJour, L. 1998. *In Defense of Pure Reason*. Cambridge: Cambridge University Press.

BonJour, L. 1999. Foundationalism and the external world. In *Philosophical Perspectives*, vol. 13, *Epistemology*, ed. J. Tomberlin, 229–249. Malden, Mass.: Blackwell.

BonJour, L. 2003a. A version of internalist foundationalism. In *Epistemic Justification: Internalism vs. Externalism, Foundations vs. Virtues*, by L. BonJour and E. Sosa, 3–96. Malden, Mass.: Blackwell.

BonJour, L. 2003b. Reply to Sosa. In *Epistemic Justification: Internalism vs. Externalism, Foundations vs. Virtues*, by L. BonJour and E. Sosa, 173–200. Malden, Mass.: Blackwell.

Brewer, T. 2002. The real problem with internalism about reasons. *Canadian Journal of Philosophy* 32:443–474.

Broad, C. D. 1923. *Scientific Thought.* New York: Harcourt Brace.

Brueckner, A. 1994. The structure of the skeptical argument. *Philosophy and Phenomenological Research* 54:827–835.

Byrne, A. 2001. Intentionalism defended. *Philosophical Review* 110:199–240.

Byrne, A., and D. Hilbert. 1997. Introduction to *Readings on Color*, vol. 1, ed. A. Byrne and D. Hilbert, xi–xviii. Cambridge, Mass.: MIT Press.

Byrne, A., and H. Logue. 2009. Introduction to *Disjunctivism: Contemporary Readings*, ed. A. Byrne and H. Logue, vii–xxix. Cambridge, Mass.: MIT Press.

Carroll, L. 1895. What the Tortoise said to Achilles. *Mind* 4:278–280.

Chalmers, D. J. 1996. *The Conscious Mind.* New York: Oxford University Press.

Chisholm, R. 1977. *The Theory of Knowledge.* 2nd ed. Englewood Cliffs, N.J.: Prentice-Hall.

Chisholm, R. 1982. *The Foundations of Knowing.* Minneapolis: University of Minnesota Press.

Cohen, S. 1984. Justification and truth. *Philosophical Studies* 46:279–295.

Cohen, S. 1998. Two kinds of skeptical argument. *Philosophy and Phenomenological Research* 58:143–159.

Conee, E., and R. Feldman. 2001. Internalism defended. In *Epistemology: Internalism and Externalism*, ed. H. Kornblith, 231–260. Oxford: Blackwell.

Crane, T. 1991. Why indeed? Papineau on supervenience. *Analysis* 51:32–37.

Davidson, D. 1986. A coherence theory of empirical knowledge. In *Truth and Interpretation*, ed. E. Lepore, 307–319. Oxford: Blackwell.

de Sousa, R. 2002. Emotional truth. *Proceedings of the Aristotelian Society* suppl. 76:247–263.

Dretske, F. 1995. *Naturalizing the Mind*. Cambridge, Mass.: MIT Press.

Evans, G. 1982. *The Varieties of Reference*. Ed. J. McDowell. Oxford: Clarendon.

Fales, E. 1996. *A Defense of the Given*. Lanham, Md.: Rowman & Littlefield.

Feldman, R. 2004. The justification of introspective beliefs. In *Evidentialism*, by E. Conee and R. Feldman, 199–218. Oxford: Clarendon.

Foster, J. 1991. *The Immaterial Self*. London: Routledge & Kegan Paul.

Foster, J. 2000. *The Nature of Perception*. Oxford: Oxford University Press.

Fumerton, R. 1995. *Metaepistemology and Skepticism*. Lanham, Md.: Rowman & Littlefield.

Gaita, R. 2000. *A Common Humanity: Thinking about Love and Truth and Justice*. London: Routledge.

Gettier, E. L. 1963. Is justified true belief knowledge? *Analysis* 23:121–123.

Goldie, P. 2000. *The Emotions: A Philosophical Exploration*. Oxford: Clarendon.

Goldman, A. I. 1979. What is justified belief? In *Justification and Knowledge*, ed. G. S. Pappas, 1–23. Dordrecht: D. Reidel.

Goldman, A. I. 1986. *Epistemology and Cognition*. Cambridge, Mass.: Harvard University Press.

Goldman, A. I. 1999. Internalism exposed. *Journal of Philosophy* 96:271–293.

Greco, J. 1999. Agent reliabilism. In *Philosophical Perspectives*, vol. 13, *Epistemology*, ed. J. Tomberlin, 273–296. Malden, Mass.: Blackwell.

Greco, J. 2000. *Putting Skeptics in Their Place*. Cambridge: Cambridge University Press.

Harman, G. 1965. Inference to the best explanation. *Philosophical Review* 74:88–95.

Harman, G. 1986. *Change in View: Principles of Reasoning.* Cambridge, Mass.: MIT Press.

Harman, G. 1990. The intrinsic quality of experience. In *Philosophical Perspectives*, vol. 4, *Action Theory and Philosophy of Mind*, ed. J. Tomberlin, 31–52. Atascadero, Calif.: Ridgeview.

Harman, G. 1996. Qualia and color concepts. In *Philosophical Issues*, vol. 7, *Perception*, ed. E. Villanueva, 75–79. Atascadero, Calif.: Ridgeview.

Hawthorne, J. 2004. Why Humeans are out of their minds. *Noûs* 38:351–358.

Heck, R. 2000. Nonconceptual content and the "space of reasons." *Philosophical Review* 109:483–523.

Helm, B. W. 2001. *Emotional Reason: Deliberation, Motivation, and the Nature of Value.* Cambridge: Cambridge University Press.

Hume, D. 1975. *Enquiries Concerning Human Understanding and Concerning the Principles of Morals.* 3rd ed. Ed. L. A. Selby-Bigge and P. H. Niddich. Oxford: Clarendon.

Hume, D. 1978. *A Treatise of Human Nature.* 2nd ed. Ed. L. A. Selby-Bigge and P. H. Niddich. Oxford: Clarendon.

Jackson, F. 1977. *Perception.* Cambridge: Cambridge University Press.

Jackson, F. 1982. Epiphenomenal qualia. *Philosophical Quarterly* 32:127–136.

Jackson, F. 1986. What Mary didn't know. *Journal of Philosophy* 83:291–295.

Jackson, F. 2004. Mind and illusion. In *There's Something About Mary: Essays on Phenomenal Consciousness and Frank Jackson's Knowledge Argument*, ed. P. Ludlow, Y. Nagasawa, and D. Stoljar, 421–442. Cambridge, Mass.: MIT Press.

John, J. 2005. Representationism, phenomenism, and the intuitive view. *Philosophical Topics* 33:159–184.

Johnston, M. 2001. The authority of affect. *Philosophy and Phenomenological Research* 63:181–214.

Johnston, M. 2004. The obscure object of hallucination. *Philosophical Studies* 120:113–183.

Kelly, S. 2001. Demonstrative concepts and experience. *Philosophical Review* 110:397–419.

Kim, J. 1998. *Mind in a Physical World.* Cambridge, Mass.: MIT Press.

Korcz, K. A. 1997. Recent work on the basing relation. *American Philosophical Quarterly* 34:171–191.

Kripke, S. A. 1980. *Naming and Necessity.* Cambridge, Mass.: Harvard University Press.

Kupperman, J. J. 2005. The epistemology of non-instrumental value. *Philosophy and Phenomenological Research* 70:659–680.

Langsam, H. 1997. The theory of appearing defended. *Philosophical Studies* 87:33–59.

Langsam, H. 2000. Experiences, thoughts, and qualia. *Philosophical Studies* 99:269–295.

Langsam, H. 2001. Strategy for dualists. *Metaphilosophy* 32:395–418.

Langsam, H. 2002. Consciousness, experience, and justification. *Canadian Journal of Philosophy* 32:1–28.

Lehrer, K. 1974. *Knowledge.* Oxford: Oxford University Press.

Lehrer, K. 1979. The Gettier problem and the analysis of knowledge. In *Justification and Knowledge*, ed. G. S. Pappas, 65–78. Dordrecht: D. Reidel.

Lewis, D. 1966. An argument for the identity theory. *Journal of Philosophy* 63:17–25.

Lewis, D. 1980. Mad pain and Martian pain. In *Readings in the Philosophy of Psychology*, vol. 1, ed. N. Block, 216–222. Cambridge, Mass.: Harvard University Press.

Lewis, D. 1986. *Philosophical Papers.* Vol. II. New York: Oxford University Press.

Lewis, D. 1995. Should a materialist believe in qualia? *Australasian Journal of Philosophy* 73:140–144.

Loar, B. 1997. Phenomenal states. In *The Nature of Consciousness*, ed. N. Block, O. Flanagan, and G. Güzeldere, 597–616. Cambridge, Mass.: MIT Press.

Locke, J. 1975. *An Essay Concerning Human Understanding.* Ed. P. H. Niddich. Oxford: Clarendon.

Lycan, W. G. 1987. *Consciousness.* Cambridge, Mass.: MIT Press.

Lycan, W. G. 1996. *Consciousness and Experience.* Cambridge, Mass.: MIT Press.

McDowell, J. 1982. Criteria, defeasibility, and knowledge. *Proceedings of the British Academy* 68:455–479.

McDowell, J. 1986. Singular thought and the extent of inner space. In *Subject, Thought, and Context*, ed. P. Pettit and J. McDowell, 137–168. Oxford: Clarendon.

McDowell, J. 1994. *Mind and World.* Cambridge, Mass.: Harvard University Press.

McDowell, J. 1995. Might there be external reasons? In *World, Mind, and Ethics: Essays on the Ethical Philosophy of Bernard Williams*, ed. J. E. J. Altham and R. Harrison, 68–85. Cambridge: Cambridge University Press.

McGinn, C. 1983. *The Subjective View.* Oxford: Clarendon.

McGinn, C. 1991. *The Problem of Consciousness.* Oxford: Blackwell.

McGinn, C. 1996. Another look at color. *Journal of Philosophy* 93:537–553.

McGinn, C. 2004. *Consciousness and Its Objects.* Oxford: Oxford University Press.

McGrew, T. J. 1995. *The Foundations of Knowledge.* Lanham, Md.: Rowman & Littlefield.

Mackie, J. 1977. *Ethics: Inventing Right and Wrong.* London: Penguin.

Marcus, D. 2001. Mental causation: Unnaturalized but not unnatural. *Philosophy and Phenomenological Research* 63:57–83.

Martin, M. G. F. 1997. Sense, reference, and selective attention II. *Proceedings of the Aristotelian Society* suppl. 71:75–98.

Martin, M. G. F. 1998. Setting things before the mind. In *Current Issues in Philosophy of Mind, Royal Institute of Philosophy Supplement 43*, ed. A. O'Hear, 157–179. Cambridge: Cambridge University Press.

Martin, M. G. F. 2004. The limits of self-awareness. *Philosophical Studies* 120:37–89.

Martin, M. G. F. 2006. On being alienated. In *Perceptual Experience*, ed. T. S. Gendler and J. Hawthorne, 354–410. Oxford: Clarendon.

Millgram, E. 1993. Pleasure in practical reasoning. *Monist* 76:394–415.

Millgram, E. 1996. Williams' argument against external reasons. *Noûs* 30:197–220.

Millikan, R. 1984. *Language, Thought, and Other Biological Categories.* Cambridge, Mass.: MIT Press.

Moore, G. E. 1903. The refutation of idealism. *Mind* 12:433–453.

Moser, P. K. 1989. *Knowledge and Evidence.* Cambridge: Cambridge University Press.

Nagel, T. 1974. What is it like to be a bat? *Philosophical Review* 83:435–450.

Nagel, T. 1986. *The View from Nowhere.* New York: Oxford University Press.

Nagel, T. 2000. The psychophysical nexus. In *New Essays on the A Priori*, ed. P. Boghossian and C. Peacocke, 433–471. Oxford: Oxford University Press.

O'Shaughnessy, B. 2000. *Consciousness and the World.* Oxford: Oxford University Press.

Papineau, D. 1993. Physicalism, consciousness, and the antipathetic fallacy. *Australasian Journal of Philosophy* 71:169–183.

Papineau, D. 1998. Mind the gap. In *Philosophical Perspectives*, vol. 12, *Language, Mind, and Ontology*, ed. J. Tomberlin, 373–388. Malden, Mass.: Blackwell.

Pautz, A. 2007. Intentionalism and perceptual presence. In *Philosophical Perspectives*, vol. 21, *Philosophy of Mind*, ed. J. Hawthorne, 495–541. Malden, Mass.: Blackwell.

Peacocke, C. 1983. *Sense and Content*. Oxford: Oxford University Press.

Peacocke, C. 2001. Does perception have a nonconceptual content? *Journal of Philosophy* 98:239–264.

Pitt, D. 2004. The phenomenology of cognition, or What is it like to think that *p*? *Philosophy and Phenomenological Research* 69:1–36.

Plantinga, A. 1990. Justification in the 20th century. *Philosophy and Phenomenological Research* suppl. 50:45–71.

Plantinga, A. 1993. *Warrant and Proper Function*. New York: Oxford University Press.

Pollock, J. L. 1986. *Contemporary Theories of Knowledge*. Totowa, N.J.: Rowman & Littlefield.

Price, H. H. 1932. *Perception*. London: Methuen.

Pritchard, D. 2005. The structure of sceptical arguments. *Philosophical Quarterly* 55:37–52.

Rachels, S. 2000. Is unpleasantness intrinsic to unpleasant experiences? *Philosophical Studies* 99:187–210.

Robinson, W. S. 2004. *Understanding Phenomenal Consciousness*. Cambridge: Cambridge University Press.

Rorty, R. 1979. *Philosophy and the Mirror of Nature*. Princeton: Princeton University Press.

Russell, B. 1911. Knowledge by acquaintance and knowledge by description. *Proceedings of the Aristotelian Society* 11:108–128.

Russell, B. 1912. *The Problems of Philosophy*. Oxford: Oxford University Press.

Scanlon, T. M. 1998. *What We Owe to Each Other*. Cambridge, Mass.: Harvard University Press.

Scheler, M. [1926] 1973. *Formalism in Ethics and Non-formal Ethics of Values*. Trans. M. S. Frings and R. L. Funk. Evanston, Ill.: Northwestern University Press.

Schueler, G. F. 1995. *Desire: Its Role in Practical Reason and the Explanation of Action*. Cambridge, Mass.: MIT Press.

Searle, J. R. 1983. *Intentionality*. Cambridge: Cambridge University Press.

Searle, J. R. 1992. *The Rediscovery of the Mind*. Cambridge, Mass.: MIT Press.

Sellars, W. 1963. Empiricism and the philosophy of mind. In *Science, Perception, and Reality*, 127–196. London: Routledge & Kegan Paul.

Shoemaker, S. 1980. Causality and properties. In *Time and Cause*, ed. P. van Inwagen, 109–135. Dordrecht: D. Reidel.

Shoemaker, S. 1986. Introspection and the self. In *Midwest Studies in Philosophy*, vol. 10, *Studies in the Philosophy of Mind*, ed. P. French, T. Uehling, and H. Wettstein, 101–120. Minneapolis: University of Minnesota Press.

Shoemaker, S. 1994. Self-knowledge and "inner sense." *Philosophy and Phenomenological Research* 54:249–314.

Shoemaker, S. 1998. Causal and metaphysical necessity. *Pacific Philosophical Quarterly* 79:59–77.

Siewert, C. P. 1998. *The Significance of Consciousness*. Princeton: Princeton University Press.

Siewert, C. P. 2004. Is experience transparent? *Philosophical Studies* 117:15–41.

Smart, J. J. C. 1959. Sensations and brain processes. *Philosophical Review* 68:141–156.

Smith, A. D. 2002. *The Problem of Perception*. Cambridge, Mass.: Harvard University Press.

Smith, M. 1994. *The Moral Problem*. Oxford: Blackwell.

Snowdon, P. 1981. Experience, vision, and causation. *Proceedings of the Aristotelian Society* 81:175–192.

Sosa, E. 1999. Skepticism and the internal/external divide. In *The Blackwell Guide to Epistemology*, ed. J. Greco and E. Sosa, 145–157. Malden, Mass.: Blackwell.

Sosa, E. 2003. Beyond internal foundations to external virtues. In *Epistemic Justification: Internalism vs. Externalism, Foundations vs. Virtues*, by L. BonJour and E. Sosa, 93–170. Malden, Mass.: Blackwell.

Sprigge, T. L. S. 1988. *The Rational Foundations of Ethics*. London: Routledge & Kegan Paul.

Sprigge, T. L. S. 1994. Consciousness. *Synthese* 98:73–93.

Stampe, D. W. 1987. The authority of desire. *Philosophical Review* 96:335–381.

Steup, M. 1999. A defense of internalism. In *The Theory of Knowledge: Classical and Contemporary Readings*, 2nd ed., ed. L. Pojman, 373–384. Belmont, Calif.: Wadsworth.

Stocker, M. 1979. Desiring the bad: An essay in moral psychology. *Journal of Philosophy* 76:738–753.

Stocker, M. 1983. Psychic feelings: Their importance and irreducibility. *Australasian Journal of Philosophy* 61:5–26.

Strawson, G. 1994. *Mental Reality*. Cambridge, Mass.: MIT Press.

Strawson, G. 2005. Intentionality and experience: Terminological preliminaries. In *Phenomenology and Philosophy of Mind*, ed. D. Smith and A. Thomasson, 41–66. Oxford: Oxford University Press.

Strawson, G. 2008. *Real Materialism and Other Essays*. Oxford: Clarendon.

Stroud, B. 1977. *Hume*. London: Routledge & Kegan Paul.

Stroud, B. 1984. *The Significance of Philosophical Scepticism*. Oxford: Clarendon.

Stubenberg, L. 1998. *Consciousness and Qualia*. Amsterdam: John Benjamins.

Swoyer, C. 1982. The nature of natural laws. *Australasian Journal of Philosophy* 60:203–223.

Thau, M. 2002. *Consciousness and Cognition*. Oxford: Oxford University Press.

Tye, M. 1992. Visual qualia and visual content. In *The Contents of Experience*, ed. T. Crane, 158–176. Cambridge: Cambridge University Press.

Tye, M. 1995. *Ten Problems of Consciousness*. Cambridge, Mass.: MIT Press.

Tye, M. 2000. *Consciousness, Color, and Content*. Cambridge, Mass.: MIT Press.

Velleman, J. D. 1992. The guise of the good. *Noûs* 26:3–26.

Wedgwood, R. 2001. Sensing values? *Philosophy and Phenomenological Research* 63:215–223.

Williams, B. 1979. Internal and external reasons. Rept. in his *Moral Luck: Philosophical Papers, 1973–1980*, 101–113. Cambridge: Cambridge University Press, 1981.

Williamson, T. 2000. *Knowledge and Its Limits*. Oxford: Oxford University Press.

Index